A Topical Study of Genesis

Albert Gardner

Copyright © 2011 Albert Gardner

All rights reserved.

Published by Pea Patch Publications
P.O. Box 9163
Chattanooga, TN 37412

Cover Illustration:
"The Light and The Word"
Copyright © 2012 April Massey McNew
P.O. Box 176
Deering, Missouri 63840

ASIN: B0054RA2WA
ISBN: 1463571720
ISBN-13: 978-1463571726

DEDICATION

To our children William, Jr., Timothy, Michael, David, and Ann Musgrave, all who believe in God, believe Him to be the creator of the world, and who respect His Holy Book. And to my partner, Frances, of fifty-nine years, the mother of our children, who had a great part in imparting these principles in the hearts of our children.

CONTENTS

CHAPTER 1 - GENESIS 1:1 1

CHAPTER 2 - THE FIRST MARRIAGE 21

CHAPTER 3 - TEMPTATION 33

CHAPTER 4 - SIN AND IT'S CONSEQUENCES 39

CHAPTER 5 - CAIN AND ABEL AND THEIR OFFERING 45

CHAPTER 6 - SIN CAUSED THE FLOOD 51

CHAPTER 7 - THE FLOOD 57

CHAPTER 8 - NOAH – A PREACHER OF RIGHTEOUSNESS 65

CHAPTER 9 - ABRAHAM A FRIEND OF GOD 75

CHAPTER 10 - LOT GOES TO SODOM 85

CHAPTER 11 - ISAAC – A CHILD OF PROMISE 91

CHAPTER 12 - JACOB THE SUPPLANTER 99

CHAPTER 13 - THE TRIALS OF JOSEPH 105

CHAPTER 14 - SOME WOMEN IN GENESIS 113

INTRODUCTION

The first verse of the Bible has been the battleground for centuries, for it reveals God as creator of the heavens and earth. Those who reject the existence of God dismiss the possibility of creation, and this requires some other explanation for the existence of the world and everything in it.

Many have rejected Ussher's date of creation because in the genealogy listed in Genesis 5, there are people skipped or missed. Bishop Ussher took the ages of those given in Genesis and figured creation was 4004 B.C.

Genealogy is not the same as chronology for they serve different purposes. Genealogy was given to trace the linage for kings, or in the case of Christ, to show He came from the proper tribe to be the Messiah. Chronology measures the time involved in a certain event, which does not concern genealogy. Though 4004 B.C. may be inaccurate for the date of creation because of gaps in genealogy in Genesis 5, it does not follow that millions of years are involved.

There are two sources of information about God. From nature we can learn about His power, existence, knowledge, and wisdom (Romans 1:20). From revelation we learn about His nature and attributes, as well as our duty to Him and our relationship to Him and others. We cannot learn what to do to be saved and how to live from things, which have been created. These matters we learn from the Bible.

Since God is the author of the Bible, and He is the creator of the world (natural science), there will be no conflict between them. The Bible is not a science book, but when it makes a scientific statement, it is always true and accurate. If the Bible and natural science contradict each other, it would mean God is at variance with Himself. The Bible does not reveal the exact time of the beginning of the world, but it did have a beginning.

The book of Genesis reveals the beginning of the unfolding of the plan of God for the human race. Adam and Eve were created with free will to choose to obey or disobey God. They chose to disobey. From that time till now, all have sinned except Christ. Sin increased so much that the earth was filled with wickedness, corruption, and violence, that God sent a worldwide flood, to destroy it.

Abraham was called and separated to begin the Jewish nation. The seed promise is traced through Abraham, Isaac and Jacob, with Jesus coming through the tribe of Judah. Joseph was sold by his brothers and taken into Egypt. In this way God saved them during the famine.

The hand of God is obvious in the history of Genesis. The beginning and care of the infant nation of Israel was so necessary for the salvation of a lost race.

All Scripture references are taken from the New King James Version unless otherwise noted.

CHAPTER 1 - GENESIS 1:1

The first verse of the Bible has been a battle ground for centuries, and will remain so. It is actually a choice between God and evolution. Those who reject the power and existence of God, usually try to explain the origin and existence of the world by some form of evolution.

The choice is clear. If one begins with God, there is plan, purpose, and wisdom, design and set goals. If one begins with evolution, there is chance, no direction or intentions, no specific expectations, haphazard, unplanned, accident, random and disorganized.

"Implicit in this verse are important statements concerning God's nature and character, statements which refute at least six fundamental heresies. The first is atheism, the view that God does not exist. The Bible offers no philosophical argument for the existence of God; it assumes His existence and views everything in the light of that assumption. The second is polytheism. The singular form of the key verb indicates that the Hebrews believed in one God and not many. There is no evidence that Israel's religion evolved from animism through polytheism and henotheism before it reached ethical monotheism. Such a suggestion is quite arbitrary and in obvious conflict with statements of Scripture. Third, this verse opposes a radical materialism, which holds matter to be eternal. Without preexisting material God brought the earth – that is, matter-into existence. Fourth, since God is clearly distinguished from His creation, this verse clearly denies pantheism. Fifth, the supernatural origin of the earth and the universe refutes naturalism; God is the Architect and Creator of all that exists. Finally, the uniqueness of this concept of origins in ancient literature makes untenable the position that special revelation is nonexistent or impossible. Human reason and inquiry, while valid, are seriously limited; the problem of origins, therefore is best solved in the light of biblical truth." Paradise to Prison – John L. Davis, page 42.

GENESIS 1:1 BEGINS WITH GOD

<u>It reveals a God who creates.</u>

There is no long argument to prove His existence, but simply states His existence. His creation demonstrates wisdom, power and planning.

Something is, therefore something always has been. Psalm 90:2 affirms God "is from everlasting to everlasting." God has always been. Some ask, "Who made God?" That is not a good question, for He is self-existent and did not have a beginning. He is the uncaused first cause. Dead lifeless matter would have to have a cause, and could not be the cause of everything else.

Jesus believed and taught creation as we read about it in Genesis 1 and 2. "Have you not read that he who made them at the beginning made them male and female" (Matthew 19:4) "But from the beginning of the creation, God made them male and female" (Mark 10:6) He did not believe they evolved, but were created as Moses stated.

<u>This verse involves the nature of the God who creates.</u>

Creation reveals His power, but it also establishes His wisdom, love and compassion. Power without benevolence produces a hated dictator who is wicked and mean to the people. God's creation shows mercy and compassion, for man is given dominion over His works (Psalms 8:6).

This verse involves the nature of man.

We are created in the image of God (Genesis 1:26). We were created and did not descend from the lower animals. "Be ye not as the horse, or as the mule, which have no understanding" (Psalm 32:9). Animals act from instinct. People act from instruction. We receive instructions, weigh the evidence, make decisions, and act on what we know.

We have in our make-up an intellect with which we can think (Proverbs 4:23, believe (Romans 10:10), understand (Matthew 13:15). We have emotions with which we can love or hate (Matthew 22:37; Hebrews 1:9). We have a will with which we can purpose (2 Corinthians 9:7), and obey (Romans 6:17-18). This is what makes us different and superior to animals, and the reason God gave man dominion over them (Psalms 8:6-8).

Though there are some similarities between man and some animals, because we have a common designer, we do not have the same flesh (1 Corinthians 15:39. We do not have the same blood (Acts 17:26).

This verse involves the diety of Christ.

Verses 1 and 2 introduce us to the trinity, though that word is not used in the text. The Hebrew word "Elohim" translated God, is plural. This would include God and Christ, and verse 2 mentions the Spirit.

The deity of Christ is connected to creation in Colossians 1:15-16. "He is the image of the invisible God, the firstborn over all creation. For by Him all things were created that are in heaven and that are on the earth, visible and invisible, whether thrones or dominions or principalities or powers. All things were created through Him and for Him. And He is before all things, and in Him all things consist."

"All things were created by Him" (John 1:3). By Christ the worlds were made (Hebrews 1:2).

Jesus was born a baby in Bethlehem to the virgin Mary

(Luke 1:30-35), and He would be called Jesus (Matthew 1:21). Isaiah 7:14 says His name would be called Immanuel, which means "God with us". Jesus had an earthly mother but a heavenly Father (Matthew 17:5).

His purpose in coming was to save the lost (Luke 19:10). He is the way, the truth, and the life (John 14:6). The scribes were right that only God can forgive (Mark 2:7). The first verse of the Bible sets the stage for His earthly work.

<u>This verse determines how we are to live and the destiny of man.</u>

Since we are made in the image of God, we started out pure and sinless, for God forms the spirit within us (Zechariah 12:1). Later verses reveal the first sin. It was the plan of God, before the foundation of the world, for Christ (the perfect Lamb), to die for sinners. Creation of man, who disobeyed God, made it necessary for the Word who was in the beginning (John 1:1) to be made man (John 1:14), and to pour out His blood so we could be saved (1 Peter 1:18-20).

The destiny of man, which is determined by the way he lives, is wrapped up in creation. Being free to choose, he is accountable for all he does.

<u>This verse explains the origin of the world as we know it.</u>

It did not evolve. It is not the result of a Big Bang. It was created. The heavens and the earth refer to the universe. "For He spoke, and it was done; He commanded, and it stood fast" (Psalms 33:9 NKJV).

"For thus says the Lord, who created the heavens, who is God, who formed the earth and made it, who has established it, who did not create it in vain, who formed it to be inhabited: I am the Lord, and there is no other: (Isaiah 45:18).

God created the earth to be inhabited. He fixed it for man, plants and animals to live on. One can see the wisdom of God in the order of things done on the different days in Genesis 1.

Dry land for man to live on, atmosphere that provides air to breathe, plants and animals for food, all appeared before Adam and Eve were created. The earth would not have been suitable for man if he had been created first. The human race would have died in its infancy.

"For the earth is the Lord's, and all its fullness" (1 Corinthians 10:26).

IT GIVES A SATISFACTORY EXPLANATION OF THE ORIGIN OF LIFE.

"The earth is the Lord's and all its fullness, the world and those who dwell therein" (Psalm 24:1). "And the Lord God formed man of the dust of the ground, and breathed into his nostrils the breath of life; and he became a living being" (Genesis 2:7).

Creation and life go hand in hand. Evolutionist have no answer to the questions about the beginning of life. Life can only come from preexisting life. Rocks and other lifeless matter can never produce life, even in 4.5 billions of years. God can create and can give life.

THIS VERSE IS NOT WITHOUT CREDIBLE SUPPORT.

Nature supports the claim that God created the world. "The heavens declare the glory of God; and the firmament shows His handiwork" (Psalms 19:1). Creation teaches us something about God. Since He is the author of the Bible, and also the source of nature, we would not expect to find a conflict between them.

"For since the creation of the world His invisible attributes are clearly seen, being understood by the things that are made, even His eternal power and Godhead, so that they are without excuse" (Romans 1:20).

"Nevertheless He did not leave Himself without witness, in that He did good, gave us rain from heaven and fruitful seasons, filling our hearts with food and gladness" (Acts 14:17).

THIS VERSE ACCEPTS THE FACT THAT MATTER IS NOT ETERNAL, BUT HAD A BEGINNING.

Before the cross, Christ prayed, "And now, O Father, glorify Me together with Yourself, with the glory which I had with You before the world was" (John 17:5). There was a time when the world did not exist.

Scientists agree that energy is not being created or destroyed, and that useable energy is becoming less available for useful work. For instance, when a tank of diesel is used to drive a truck, it is changed into gases, but cannot be used for that purpose again. When coal is burned, it is changed to ashes and gases, but it cannot be used like that again. When uranium has finished giving off energy, that which is left is lead, and cannot be used for energy again.

"God created the heavens and the earth." "By faith we understand that the worlds were framed by the word of God, so that the things which are seen were not made of things which are visible" (Hebrews 11:3).

IF WE REJECT THIS VERSE AS A TRUE HAPPENING, THERE ARE SERIOUS CONSEQUENCES.

Belief in a God who creates, gives a standard for morality. If there is no God, we are not accountable for how we live. There is no standard to measure actions.

On what basis can we say it is wrong for a wicked dictator to kill thousands of his people? It would not be wrong if there is no standard by which we can know what is right or wrong.

The conclusion Solomon reached is right. "Let us hear the conclusion of the whole matter: Fear God and keep His commandments, For this is man's all. For God will bring every work into judgment, including every secret thing, whether good or evil" (Ecclesiastes 12:13-14).

"And there is no creature hidden from His sight, but all things are naked and open to the eyes of Him to whom we must give account" (Hebrews 4:13).

"The eyes of the Lord are in every place, keeping watch on the evil and the good" (Proverbs 16:2).

THIS VERSE GIVES CREDIBILITY TO OTHER BIBLE BOOKS.

Paul reveals the nature of the unknown God at Athens. "God, who made the world and everything in it, since He is Lord of heaven and earth, does not dwell in temples made with hands" (Acts 17:24).

When men were intending to offer a burnt sacrifice to Paul and Barnabas, Paul asked, "Men, Why are you doing these things? We also are men with the same nature as you, and preach to you that you should turn from these useless things to the living God, who made the heaven, the earth, the sea, and all things that are in them" (Acts 14:15).

This verse remains the battleground between Creation and evolution. Honesty in dealing with these matters demands we consider all the evidence available. When we put truth and error side by side, we can easily tell the difference.

Jesus taught that anyone who really wanted to do His will, can find it. "If anyone wills to do His will, he shall know concerning the doctrine, whether it is from God or whether I speak on My own authority" (John 7:17).

LENGTH OF DAYS IN GENESIS 1

The word "day" is used in different ways in the Bible. "Today is the day of Salvation" (2 Corinthians 6:1). "The day of the Lord". This does not refer to a twenty-four hour day. Jesus fasted for "forty" days and forty nights" (Matthew 4:2). We understand that to mean forty solar days of twenty-dour hours each and not long periods of time. Jonah was in the whale's belly three days and three nights. We understand that to mean three ordinary days of twenty-four hours each, and not long periods of time.

In Genesis 1 we read of the first day with its evening and

morning. Then, the second on through the seventh day. Were it not an attempt to fit the Theory of Evolution into this chapter, we would all understand these days to mean twenty-four hour days. Because the Theory of Evolution demands long periods of time, the claim is made that the days of this chapter refer to long periods of time, maybe even a million years each. There are good reasons to reject this idea, and to accept the view that the days in Genesis 1 are twenty-four hour days.

When a number is put before day, it refers to a twenty-four day. Jesus certainly did not fast a million years, but only forty solar days. Jonah was not in the belly of the fish three million years, for day in Jonah 1:17 refers to a twenty-four hour day.

If the days in Genesis 1 are as much as a million years each, that would mean approximately half of that time would be light and half would be dark. On the third day God said "let there be grass, herb, and fruit trees." These could not live without light, so during the half million years of darkness all plant life would die.

Adam was created on the sixth day. If that day was a million years, Adam would be at least a half million years old. Actually, ALL the days of Adam were nine hundred and thirty years (Genesis 5:5). The number before the years indicate we are to accept it in the normal length of time.

When Moses listed the Ten Commandments, he refers to creation. The Jews were to do no work on the Sabbath. "For in six days the Lord made the heavens and the earth, the sea, and all that is in them, and rested on the seventh day. Therefore the Lord blessed the Sabbath day and hallowed it"" (Exodus 20:11).

The Jews understood the Sabbath to be a twenty-four hour day, rather than a long period of time. They were to do their work in six days and the seventh day was the Sabbath (Deuteronomy 5:13-14). All of these were normal days.

The only reason to make the six days of creation (Exodus 20:11), anything other than normal solar days, is to make Genesis fit the Theory of Evolution. It is a compromise with a

A Topical Study of Genesis

false theory.

2 Peter 3:8 is used by some to claim the days of Genesis 1 are at least a thousand years. The context of this verse is the second coming of Christ. The scoffers were saying that since His coming was delayed, that was evidence He was not coming.

Peter states things have not continued as they were from creation and gives the flood as evidence. "But, beloved, do not forget this one thing, that with the Lord one day is as a thousand years, and a thousand years as one day." It simply means God's timetable is not like ours, and that the delay shows the longsuffering of God, which will allow more people to repent and be saved (2 Peter 3:9,15).

Even if the days of Genesis 1 were one thousand years, it would mean five hundred years of darkness in which plants, animals and man could not survive.

THE TRINITY

The word "trinity" does not appear in the Bible, but the fact that there are three members of Deity is clearly taught in scripture.

Instead of trinity, the Holy Spirit uses the word Godhead. When Paul preached against idols in Athens, he used this word. "Forasmuch then as we are the offspring of God, we ought not to think that the Godhead is like unto gold, or silver, or stone, graven by art and man's device" (Acts 17:29 KJV).

Paul writes about the nature of Christ in Colossians 2:9. "For in Him dwells all the fullness of the Godhead bodily". The Godhead consists of the Father, Son and Holy Spirit. All three of them are often mentioned in the same verse.

When Jesus was baptized, the Godhead was present (Matthew 13: 13-17). Jesus was in the water, the Spirit descended on Him like a dove, and the heavenly Father said, "This is My Son, in whom I am well pleased.

Matthew's account of the Great Commission, Jesus tells the apostles to "Go therefore and make disciples of all nations, baptizing them in the name of the Father and of the Son and of the Holy Spirit" (Matthew 28:19).

Jesus had promised He would send the Holy Spirit on them (John 14:16). When He reminds them of this promise He mentions all three members of the Godhead. "But when the Helper comes, whom I shall send to you from the Father, the Spirit of truth who proceeds from the Father, He will testify of me" (John 15:29).

Hebrews 9 gives a contrast of some thing under the law, and says they are symbolic of some things under the gospel (verse 9). One thing is pointed out that the sacrifices of animals could not cleanse the conscience. Only the blood of Christ could do that. Notice the Godhead in connection with blood of Christ. "How much more shall the blood of Christ, who through the eternal Spirit offered Himself without spot to God, cleanse your conscience from dead works to serve the living God?" (Hebrews 9:14).

The teaching that there are three Persons in the Godhead is fully developed in the New Testament as we have seen from the above verses, but it is also taught in the first chapter of Genesis.

The Hebrew word Elohim, translated God in verse one, is plural. This would include God and Christ. The second verse says the "Spirit of God was hovering over the face of the waters." In these two versed we observe the three Persons in the Godhead.

We may not understand how there can be three, yet one. We can believe it, even if we don't understand it. We may not understand electricity but we believe it works for us. We may not understand gravity, but we know it works. The Bible teaches three Persons in the Godhead, so we believe it, knowing "His ways past finding out" (Romans 11:33).

GOD IS

The evidence for the existence of God is great. The Bible begins with God. We believe in God because we believe the Bible. Is the Bible true? Can we rely on it? Does it give a credible account of events?

A Topical Study of Genesis

If the Bible is true, then what it says about God is also true. "But without faith it is impossible to please Him, for he who comes to God must believe that He is, and that He is a rewarder of those who diligently seek Him" (Hebrews 11:6).

There is irrefutable evidence for the inspiration of the Bible. It is of such a nature that it could not have come from unaided man.

WE BELIEVE THE BIBLE BECAUSE OF FULFILLED PROPHECY.

Prophecies were given sometimes hundreds of years before the event, yet they were fulfilled to the letter and were exact. The Bible writers could not have known unless it was revealed to them.

Everest said, "the farther the event from the time when the prophet lived the more sure the indication of divine oversight." The prophet stated it right when he said God could, "declare the end from the beginning" (Isaiah 46:10).

THE FINDINGS OF ARCHAEOLOGY SUPPORT THE BIBLE ACCOUNT IN EVERY INSTANCE.

The science of Archaeology is the study of material remains of past human life and activities. If a city is buried, and much later is uncovered, what will they find? They will find exactly what existed when the city was covered with dirt. Nothing has been added. It will tell the truth about the past.

Haley gives the following example concerning the bricks of Pithom. When the Jews were in Egypt as slaves they were required to make bricks for the city of Pithom and were provided with straw each day. In order to punish them and make their tasks more difficult, Pharoah forced them to gather their own straw, and they were to make the same number of bricks as before. (Exodus 5:10). What one would expect to find in the bricks centuries later would be exactly what they did in making bricks.

"Naville, 1883, and Kyle, 1908, found, at Pithom, the lower courses of brick filled with good chopped straw; the middle courses, with less straw, and that was stubble plucked up by the root; and the upper courses of brick were of pure clay, having no straw whatever. What an amazing confirmation of the Exodus account." Handbook, page 117.

One of the ten plaques on Egypt before the Jews were permitted to leave, was the death of their first born including the first born of Pharaoh (Exodus 12:29-30). Halley makes mention of this in Pharaoh's lineage.

"Inscriptions have been found indicating that Thothmes IV, successor of Amenhotep 11, was not his first-born nor heir apparent. Also, that Merneptah's first-born met death in peculiar circumstances, and his whichever the Pharaoh, the Biblical statement is confirmed." Handbook, page 119.

THERE IS NO CONFLICT BETWEEN TRUE BIBLE TEACHING AND TRUE SCIENCE.

The Bible is not a science book, but when it makes a scientific statement, it is always true and up to date. God is the authority of both nature and the Bible, so they will be saying the same thing.

Only in recent years have people concluded the earth is round, yet the Bible has so stated it long ago, when it says, "It is He who sits above the circle of the earth" (Isaiah 40:22).

Some have thought the earth in the shoulders of Atlas on the back of a huge turtle. Now we understand something about the principle of gravity, which the Bible stated in Job 26:7. "He hangs the earth on nothing."

Astronomers know there is a place in the North where there are no stars. "He stretches out the north over empty space" (Job 26:7).

One time when Matthew Fontaine Maury was sick, his son read to him, where it says there are Paths in the sea. (Psalms 8) He said, "If the word of God says there are paths in the sea, they must be there. I will find them. "After a few years he had charted the paths in the sea, which are followed by ships even today.

A Topical Study of Genesis

WE BELIEVE THE BIBLE BECAUSE OF ITS UNITY.

From first to last, the Bible writers were separated by about 1600 years, yet there is a unity that cannot be explained other than by a Guiding Hand over the Bible writers. Most of them did not know one another, so there could be no conspiracy, especially since they separated by so much time and distance. When the book from about forty different writers are brought together, there is no conflict and they speak with one voice.

Secular writers contradict each other on the same subject, and often disagree with their own earlier writings. The Bible from beginning to end is the story of redemption.

THE THEORY OF EVOLUTION

In 1859, Charles Darwin published his book, <u>The Origin of The Species</u>, which has made tremendous changes in science and religion. The battle between creation and evolution is unending and unyielding.

Evolution is presented and accepted by many as fact. There is so much hatred of God and the Bible, that any mention of creation as a possible explanation for the origin of the universe is forbidden. Actually, if one accepts either creation or evolution, regardless of supporting evidence, they must be accepted by faith.

There are similarities between plants and between animals including man. That is obvious, but all that proves is that they have a common designer.

According to evolution, man descended from an ape like animal. We are just an advanced animal because we can talk. This is not true because we do not have the same blood as animals. We cannot take a blood transfusion from a monkey.

"And He has made from one blood every nation of men to dwell on all the face of the earth, and has determined their preappointed times and the boundaries of their dwellings" (Acts 17:26).

Not only do we not have the same blood as animals, we do not have the same flesh. "All flesh is not the same flesh, but there is one kind of flesh of men, another flesh of animals, another of fish, and another of birds" (1 Corinthians 15:39). We have a common maker and designer, but we did not come from the lower animals.

FOSSILS

Fossil is defined as, "a remnant, impression, or trace of an animal or plant of past geological ages that has been preserved in the earth's crust."

Fossils tell the story of the past. The great number of fossils which have been preserved, do not support the evolutionary theory. The claim is made that over a period of millions of years, changes took place where animals from the sea changed into land animals. One kind of animal became another.

If that were true, what would the fossil record show? We should find fossils of those in-between stages, but none exist. We should find fossils of one that is not like the one it came from, and different from the one it is to become. There are no transitional fossils.

It is unscientific to say one species can change into another. In order to prove animals are changing, pictures of horses are shown, some large, some very small, with many in-between. That kind of change is admitted, but that is not the meaning of evolution. There may be many sizes of horses, but they are still horses. Horses do not become elephants.

There are dozens of breeds of dogs, but they are still dogs, and they never become cats. It was established in the beginning that everything would bring forth after its kind. What evolutionists must find are fossils, which record the change from one animal to another. Those fossils do not exist, which means it did not happen.

FROM THE SIMPLE TO THE COMPLEX

The claim is made that in evolution, the change is from the simple to the complex. Beginning with one cell, it evolved after millions of years to the human body with the various complex nervous system, blood system and digestive system. However, the reverse of this actually happens.

Hogs that are brought to a high stage of development, when they are turned into the wild, don't become better, but decline and take on undesirable traits. According to evolution they should get better and better.

Concerning man, we are supposed to be getting better with time. But is it true? "But evil men and imposters will grow worse and worse, deceiving and being deceived" (2 Timothy 3:15). According to evolution we started out way down and are getting better. According to the Bible we began in a perfect state before sin, and we fell.

LIFE CAME FROM LIFE

It is an accepted fact that life can only come from pre-existing life. Evolutionists begin with matter, because the only other option in mind, actually God. However, matter had a beginning, for it is not eternal.

The theory of evolution, does not allow for the beginning of life, and cannot explain how lifeless dead matter can give life. Even with billions of years this could not happen. Life comes from life.

Something is, therefore something has always been. There are only two options: either matter or mind. If that something that has always been, was matter, how can you explain the origin of life? Where did male and female originate? When did the conscience come into being?

If there was an explosion called the Big Bang, how did conditions arrive that could produce such an explosion caused purely by matter with no power to plan, organize or have power over conditions?

If it is claimed that an explosion followed established laws, we must ask, where did the laws come from? What laws and what power could produce conditions that would cause an explosion? A law implies a law-giver. Who is the law-giver? Laws do not make themselves.

There may be some unanswered questions with this starting point, but the major questions will be answered. Evolution or creation must be accepted by faith.

Albert Gardner

THEISTIC EVOLUTION

Some Bible believers have caved in to the pressure of evolutionists, and have become "theistic evolutionists." They have compromised by saying both are true. They claim God created the world, but He did it through the process of evolution.

We have already shown evolution is unscientific, and evidence from fossils do not support the theory of evolution. Another reason theistic evolution cannot be accepted, is because there are conflicts between creation and evolution. Logically we cannot accept contradictory teaching.

In order to accept evolution as the way God created the world, one would have to establish that evolution is credible.

Creation teaches life came only from pre-existing life. Everything would bring forth after its kind (Genesis 1:11). Evolution begins with lifeless matter, and cannot account for the beginning of matter, and certainly not the beginning of life.

Man was created from the dust of the ground (Genesis 2:7). Evolution holds that man descended from an ape like animal.

Evolution teaches life and animals originate in the water, but the Bible teaches they began on land (Genesis 1:9-12; 24-25).

Evolution cannot account for: the origin of matter, origin of the earth and the order and unity in it, the origin of life, origin of the species, the development of organs of the body, the sexes, the conscience, or the plan of history resulting in a Redeemer. The Bible allows for all of these.

Gospel preacher, Tom Dockery, deceased, gave ten areas where Theistic Evolution is not in harmony with the Bible.

It disagrees with the Bible on the creation of both man and woman Genesis 1:26; 2:7, 21-23.

It disagrees with the Bible on the high civilized state of man in the beginning.

It usually says that life began in the water but the Bible says it began on land –Genesis 1:11.

It disagrees with the Bible on the high moral and religious

nature of man from the beginning —Genesis 4:3, 4; Hebrews 11:4.

It says you do not necessarily reap what you have sown but may get something else —Genesis 1:11, 12, 21, 24; Galatians 6:7.

It disagrees with the teaching of Hebrews 11:3 which states, "that things which are seen were not made of things which do appear."

It has no purpose if you accept the all powerful God of the Bible.

There is no evidence for it either in science or the Bible.

It doesn't take into consideration the powerful influence of the flood on the earth.

It destroys faith in the Bible – Romans 10:17.

CREATION OF EVE

God said, "it is not good" for man to be alone. He caused a deep sleep to fall on Adam, and He took from his side a rib and made Eve as a helper, one suitable or corresponding to him. When men are left alone, they may become hardened and harsh. They need the sensitive nature of a woman to calm them and mellow their spirits, which helps to develop in them compassion and kindness.

The bone was not taken from the head of Adam to indicate she is to rule over him. Neither was the bone taken from his foot suggesting he would trample on her. The bone was taken from his side, to indicate she is by his side as an equal where he can love, provide for and protect her.

Davis lists five lessons we can learn about marriage from the creation of Adam and Eve.

Marriage was instituted by God (Genesis 2:22-24).

Marriage is to be monogamous; God gave Adam just one wife. Polygamy and divorce existed "but from the beginning it was not so" (Matthew 19:8).

Marriage is to be heterosexual; the mate whom God created for Adam, a male, was Eve, a female.

The husband and wife are to be unified physically and

spiritually, knit together by love and mutual respect (Genesis 2:24; Matthew 19: 4).

The husband is to be the head of the wife. She is a partner, one who compliments and corresponds to him. (pp 78-79).

The headship of man is based on the fact that Adam was created first (1 Timothy 2:13; 1 Corinthians 11:8,9). This is not a cultural matter, for Paul connects this teaching to creation.

The husband is the head, but he does not rule as a dictator. "Husbands, love your wives, just as Christ also loved the church and gave Himself for her" (Ephesians 5:25). When the husband displays proper love in his family, the wife and children will not find it difficult to follow his lead.

In some ways husbands and wives are equals, but in another sense he is head. This does not mean she is inferior, for in fact, she may be superior in some ways. She may know more. She may be stronger in faith and will. Her home life and background may be better. We recognize his headship because God instituted it that way.

AGE OF THE EARTH

"In the beginning God created the heavens and the earth" (Genesis 1:1). There was a beginning. The universe was created in the beginning, but the Bible does not reveal when this happened.

ArchBishop Ussher (1580-1656) added the ages of those mentioned in the Bible and figured creation was 4004 B.C. Because genealogy is not the same as Chronology, many reject Ussher's date, and point out there are some names that are skipped in the genealogical record. (Compare Ezra 7:3-4 and 1 Chronicles 6:6-10).

It may be that some names are omitted, so Ussher's date may be inaccurate. However, even allowing for some omissions, some believe the date could be no more than about ten thousand years.

Involved in this question also, is the age of man on the earth. When Jesus was answering a question about divorce, He takes them back to the beginning to show them how God intended marriage. "But from the beginning of the creation, God made them male and female" (Mark 10:6).

Human beings were created from the beginning. From Genesis 1 we learn Adam and Eve were created on the sixth day. Man did not evolve but was created from the beginning. This means the heavens and earth are the same age as man.

Evolutionists claim the earth is 4.5 billion years old, and came about by chance with life coming from lifeless matter.

The real issue is not the exact age of the earth, but who caused the earth to exist. The Bible answer is that God created it. He created it with wisdom and purpose. He formed it to be inhabited (Isaiah 45:18). The order of the things done on the days of creation show the wisdom of God. Man was created on the sixth day after there was light, air and food. If man had been created the first day, he could not have survived.

GAP THEORY

The Gap Theory is the idea that there is a gap of time between Genesis 1:1 and Genesis 1:2. Davis explains the meaning of theory in his commentary on Genesis.

"The gap theory, as generally taught today, asserts that in the dateless past God created a perfect heaven and earth. The earth was inhabited by a pre-Adamic race and who dwelt in the Garden of Eden. Satan desired to become like God and eventually rebelled (Isaiah 14). Thus sin entered the universe, and God's judgment came in the form of first a great flood and then, when the light and heat from the sun ended, a global ice age. All plant, animal, and human fossils date from this great flood and are genetically unrelated to plants, animals and humans on the earth today." According to this view, Genesis 1 is the renewal of the earth, not the creation of it.

There is no biblical or scientific evidence for a "civilization" before Adam who was the first man. :And so it is written, the first man Adam became a living being. The last Adam became a life giving spirit" (1 Corinthians 15:45). The first Adam is the one mentioned in Genesis 2:7, and the one who was the type of Christ, the second Adam (Romans 5:14). It is pure speculation and imagination to put forth a civilization before Adam. How could he be the first man if there were people before him? This view is another attempt to accommodate the evolutionary agenda and allow for millions of years between verses 1 and 2. No other Bible passage alludes to people before the creation (Matthew 19:4; Mark 10:6; John 17:5; 1 Peter 1:20; 2 Peter 3:4).

In some English translations, in Genesis 1:28, God told Adam to "replenish" the earth. That would imply there had been other people and he is to replenish the earth. The correct translation to the Hebrew word is "fill", not replenish.

Those who believe the gap theory, distinguish the words "create" and "make". That is, God created, but He also made things out of what had been created. This would leave room for many years between creation and that which was made. However, the Bible uses these words to mean the same thing (Exodus 20:11; Genesis 2:3; Nehemiah 9:6; Genesis 1:21,25). It is certainly true that God created Adam (Genesis 1:27), but He made him out of the dust of the ground (Genesis 2:7). God created and made the heavens and the earth (Exodus 20:11; Genesis 1:1).

CHAPTER 2 - THE FIRST MARRIAGE

Adam, the first man (1 Corinthians 15:45), was created from the dust of the ground, and God "breathed into his nostrils the breath of life; and man became a living being" (Genesis 2:7).

God said, "It is not good that man should be alone; I will make him a helper comparable to him" (Genesis 2:18). The animals passed before Adam when he named them and among them there was not found a suitable helper for Adam. God caused a deep sleep to fall on Adam, and He took a rib and made woman and brought her to Adam.

And Adam said, "This is now bone of my bones and flesh of my flesh; She shall be called woman because she was taken out of man" (Genesis 2:23).

And God said, "Therefore a man shall leave his father and mother and be joined to his wife, and they shall become one flesh"(Genesis 2:24). Jesus quotes this verse and attributes it to God (Matthew 19:4-5). That statement did not come from Adam, but from God.

THE NEED TO STUDY

It is important that we study about marriage and the family because without proper knowledge we will often live in opposition to God's plan for us. Divorce is a growing social problem. Many divorce and remarry when they have no right to do so. Young people, growing up, need to be taught about the home, as God would have it. We must not fail the children.

A failure to teach on this Bible subject is inexcusable. Friends or loved ones who are living in sin does not change Bible teaching. Gibbons, who wrote "The Rise and Fall of the Roman Empire", gave as one reason for the fall of the Roman Empire, the rapid increase of divorce, with the undermining of the sacctity of the home, which is the basis of society.

ORIGIN OF THE HOME

There are three divine institutions: the home, civil government (Romans 17:1) and the church (Matthew 16:18). The home is first, and existed long before the church, so marriage is not a church ordinance. That means the divine rules for marriage are for everyone, and not just for those in the church.

Marriage is for the human race. In the beginning God told Adam, "A man shall leave his father and mother". There was no real sense in which Adam could do that, so these instructions were for all people.

Before the flood came people were "marrying and giving in marriage" until the very day Noah entered the ark. It is obvious these marriages were between people who were not in the church (Matthew 23:38).

Herod was certainly not a Christian, for he lived before the church began. "For Herod himself has sent and laid hold of John, and bound him in prison for the sake of Herodias, his brother Philip's wife; for he had married her. Because John had said to Herod, "It is not lawful for you to have your brother's wife" (Mark 6:17-18).

It was not lawful. It was against God's law. He had married his brother's wife but he had no right to do so, which means he was living in adultery. This example shows us that marriage laws are for the human race, and not just for Christians.

People are obligated to learn what pleases God, and unless they do they may find themselves in an unscriptural marriage which must be dissolved in order to please God. The Jews had to put away their foreign wives (Nehemiah 13:23-27) in order to restore true religion.

There are only three classes of people who have a right to marry and have the blessings of God.

Those who have never been married and are physically fit and are mentally alert.

Those whose companion is dead.

Those whose companion has committed fornication.

MARRIAGE ORIGINATED WITH GOD.

He said of Adam, "It is not good that man should be alone; I will make him a helper comparable to him" (Genesis 2:18). Eve was the other half. She was suitable to him. She completed him.

Marriage is honorable among all, and the bed undefiled; but fornicators and adulterers God will judge" (Hebrews 13:4). One mark of those who have departed from the faith, is they will "forbid to marry" (1 Timothy 4:3). No one has a right to forbid what God allows.

Marriage is permissible, but not mandatory. One can be a Christian and be pleasing to God and choose not to marry. The apostle Paul was not married, but understood not everyone could live a pure single life (1 Corinthians 7:6-9). Some become eunuchs for the sake of the kingdom (Matthew 19:12). People do not have to marry but if they do they must follow scriptural teaching.

It is not always expedient to marry. There may be circumstances that would make it unwise to marry, or at least to postpone it. Paul advised the Corinthians on this matter. "I suppose therefore that this is good because of the present distress – that it is good for a man to remain as he is" (1 Corinthians 7:26). We do not know what that "present distress" was, but his readers knew. He continues in verse 28, to tell them they do not sin if they marry, but he was trying to spare them trouble by waiting until the present distress has passed.

PURPOSES OF MARRIAGE

Since marriage is from God, we can be sure it is for our good and for His glory. He also sets the purposes and states the duties of marriage and the family. Much of our happiness and usefulness in life will be determined by our relationship in marriage, especially as to whether we live according to divine purposes.

1. REPRODUCTION

When the animals passed before Adam, none were suitable to him for reproduction. Having sex with animals is sinful and forbidden. "If a man mates with an animal, he shall surely be put to death, and you shall kill the animal" (Leviticus 20:15).

Sex is normal, but it is to be expressed only within marriage (Matthew 5:28). Reproduction would not be possible if male and female were not attracted to one another. Without reproduction, the human family would disappear from the earth. God has placed within us certain urges or appetites for our good. If we had no desire for food and water and neglected to eat and drink we would die. Poison food is forbidden if we are to have good health. Those good appetites must be controlled by us, if we are to please God. In the same way sexual desire is normal, but must be controlled and satisfied within marriage.

2. ANOTHER PURPOSE FOR MARRIAGE IS TO PREVENT IMMORALITY

In reply to a question Paul answers, "Now concerning the things of which you wrote to me: It is good for a man not to touch a woman. Nevertheless, because of sexual immorality, let each man have his own wife, and let each woman have her own husband" (1 Corinthians 7:1-2).

The Greek word for sexual immorality is pornea, and includes fornication, adultery, homosexuality, having sex with an animal, and any other kind of forbidden sexual activity.

Do not deprive one another except with consent for a time, that you may give yourselves to fasting and prayer; and come together again so that Satan does not tempt you because of your lack of self-control" (1 Corinthians 7:5). People can express normal sexual urges within marriage, which eliminates the need to do so in any unscriptural way.

3. Marriage provides companionship

God said of Adam, "It is not good that man should be alone; I will make him a helper comparable to him" (Genesis 2:18). Adam was alone and lonely. One of the most difficult adjustments that must be made when one's companion dies, is the problem of loneliness.

4. Marriage will share work.

Eve was given to Adam as his helper. Young widows are to "marry, bear children, manage the house, give no opportunity to the adversary to speak reproachfully" (1 Timothy 5:14). This divides the work, so it does not fall on one person.

5. Marriage is designed for children

Children are from God. "Behold, children are a heritage

from the Lord, The fruit of the womb is a reward. Like arrows in the hand of a warrior, so are the children of one's youth. Happy is the man who has his quiver full of them; they shall not be ashamed, but shall speak with their enemies in the gate" (Psalm 127:3-5).

God places the production, care and training of children with parents. That duty does not belong to civil government, or even to the church, but belongs to fathers and mothers. Jewish parents were instructed about constantly teaching their children.

"You shall love the Lord your God with all your heart with all your soul, and with all your strength. And these words which I command you today shall be in your heart. You shall teach them diligently to your children, and shall talk of them when you sit in your house, when you walk by the way, when you lie down, and when you rise up. You shall bind them as a sign on your hand, and they shall be as frontlets between your eyes. Yoou shall write them on the doorposts of your house and on your gates" (Deuteronomy 6:5-9).

A failure to teach one generation results in a departure from God and His way. "So the people served the Lord all the days of Joshua, and all the days of the elders who outlived Joshua, who had seen all the great works of the Lord which He had done for Israel... What all that generation had been gathered to their fathers, another generation arose after them who did not know the Lord nor the work which He had done for Israel" (Judges 2:7, 10). Someone failed to teach the coming generation.

The duty of one generation to the next one is clear. "That the generation to come might know them, the children who would be born, that they may arise and declare them to their children, that they may set their hope in God, and not forget the works of God, but keep His commandments; and may not be like their fathers, a stubborn and rebellious generation, a generation that did not set its heart aright, and whose spirit was not faithful to God"(Psalm 78:6-8).

Christian parents must be diligent in teaching their children.

"And you fathers, do not provoke your children to wrath, but bring them up in the training and admonition of the Lord" (Ephesians 6:4). Correction and instruction must be administered in such a way, that the children will not be discouraged (Colossians 3:21).

Children are from God. It is sad when women refuse to bear children and resort to abortion.

Abortion is sinful because it is the taking of human life. Hugo McCord stated, "The fertilized egg on day one has 46 chromosomes which forever fix each organ of the adult human being." From conception life begins, "and all changes are merely stages of development." Life begins at conception.

God tells Jeremiah about his appointed work. "Before I formed you in the womb I knew you; before you were born I sanctified you; I ordained you a prophet to the nations" (Jeremiah 1:5). If his mother had aborted Jeremiah, it would have prevented the work of God through this great prophet.

Seven things that God hates are listed in Proverbs 6:16-17. One is that God hates "hands that shed innocent blood". Surely abortion would be included as an unborn baby is destroyed.

Mary went to visit Elizabeth, "and it happened, when Elizabeth heard the greeting of Mary, that the babe leaped in her womb" (luke 1:41). The angels informed the shepherds about the birth of Jesus. "And this will be the sign to you. You will find a Babe wrapped in swaddling cloths, lying in a manger" (Luke 2:12). Jesus is a "babe" after birth, and John is a "babe" before birth. When women have an abortion, they abort a baby.

WHAT DO YOU THINK?

A professor at the UCLA medical school asked his students this question: "Here is the family history: the father has syphilis. The mother has TB. They already have four children. The first is blind. The second has died. The third is deaf. The fourth has TB. The mother is pregnant. The parents are willing to have an abortion if you decide they should. What do you think? Most of the students decided on abortion. "Congratulations," said Professor Agnew, "You have just murdered Beethoven."

WHAT GOD INTENDED

HE INTENDED THAT THERE BE ONE COMPANION

"Nevertheless because of sexual immorality, let each man have his own wife, and let each woman have her own husband" (1 Corinthians 7:2).

HE INTENDED IT FOR THIS LIFE

"For in the resurrection they neither marry nor are given in marriage, but are like angels of God in heaven" (Matthew 22:30).

HE INTENDED IF FOR LIFE

"For the woman who has a husband is bound by the law to her husband as long as he lives. But the husband dies, she is released from the law of her husband"(Romans 7:2). "A wife is bound by law as long as her husband lives; but if her husband dies, she is at liberty to be married to whom she wishes, only in the Lord" (1 Corinthians 7:39).

THERE IS ONE EXCEPTION

"And I say to you, whoever divorces his wife, except for sexual immorality, and marries another, commits adultery; and whoever marries her who is divorced commits adultery" (Matthew 19:9).

A Topical Study of Genesis

WHAT IS THE "PAULINE PRIVILEGE" IN 1 CORINTHIANS 7:15?

Some refer to this verse to say that Paul is giving desertion as another cause for remarriage of the one who is deserted, while the one who deserted is still living. We should look at the whole context and analyze it.

1 Corinthians 7:10-15 Now to the married I command, yet not I but the Lord: A wife is not to depart from her husband. 11. But even if she does depart, let her remain unmarried or be reconciled to her husband. And a husband is not to divorce his wife. 12. But to the rest I, not the Lord, say: If any brother has a wife sho does not believe, and she is willing to live with him, let him not divorce her. 13 And a woman who has a husband who does not believe, if he is willing to live with her, let her not divorce him. 14. For the unbelieving husband is sanctified by the wife, and the unbelieving wife is sanctified by the husband;; otherwise your children would be unclean, but now they are holy. 15. But if the unbeliever departs, let him depart; a brother or a sister is not under bondage in such cases. But God has called us to peace.

Roy H. Lanier, Sr. points out several lessons we should gain from these verses.

1. The union of a believer is a holy union and should not be broken.

2. The believer is not to leave the unbeliever.

3. This context does not deal with two Christians, but with a Christian married to an unbeliever.

4. The Lord's law of marriage is binding upon alien sinners.

The believer is not obligated to leave Christ to preserve the marriage (Luke 14:26). This is not an example that teaches one he should marry outside the church. There are many good reasons why Christians should marry Christians.

The case before us is of two unbelievers who are married to each other, and one hears and obeys the gospel but the other does not.

What is the duty of the Christian in this matter? Hear Paul: "Let not the wife depart from her husband" (verse 10). Let him not put her away (verse 12). There will be obvious differences, but the Christian will stay and try to work out the problems and preserve the marriage. The same teaching is given to the Christian husband who has an unbelieving wife.

In the event that it is necessary for her to depart in order to live the Christian life, her duty is spelled out very clearly. "But and if she depart, let her remain unmarried, or be reconciled to her husband". And let not the husband put away his wife" (verse 11). 1. She is to remain unmarried and live a single life, or, 2. Be reconciled to her husband. Remarriage to someone else is not mentioned and is not given as an option.

In Romans 7:2, marriage is used to illustrate we are not under the law of Moses. "For the woman which hath a husband is bound by the law to her husband so long as he liveth; but if the husband be dead, she is loosed from the law of her husband." Notice two words: bound and loosed.

In 1 Corinthians 7:27, 39, the same Greek word is used in connection with marriage. "Bound unto a wife", and "wife bound by the law as long as her husband liveth."

However, in 1 Corinthians 7:15, a different Greek word is used. "A brother or sister is not under bondage in such cases." Romans 7:2 says they are bound, while 1 Corinthians 7:15 says they are not under bondage. Thayer defines bondage as "to make a slave of, reduce to bondage. Concerning 1 Corinthians 7:15 he says, "to be under bondage, held by constraint of law or necessity in some matter." A brother or sister has never been a slave or in bondage to any man in this sense.

If the unbeliever is unwilling to live with the Christian unless they give up their faith and the practice of Christianity,

Paul says, "let them depart." A Christian must not give up his faith in order to preserve the marriage (Luke 14:26).

From <u>Your Marriage Can Be Great</u> by Thomas B. Warren

Albert Gardner

CHAPTER 3 - TEMPTATION

Temptation is not sin, for Christ "was in all points tempted as we are, yet without sin" (Hebrews 4:15). It is yielding to temptation that is sin. "Who committed no sin, nor was deceit found in His mouth" (1 Peter 2:22).

Though Jesus did not yield to temptation, it is obvious that all of us did yield and became sinners (Romans 3:23; 1 John 1:8,10).

TWO KINDS OF TEMPTATION

Abraham was tested (tempted KJV) when he was told to offer Isaac as a sacrifice (Genesis 22:1). All of us will be tested to be sure our faith is genuine (1 Peter 1:6-7). Abraham passed the test, for the angel of the Lord said, "Do not lay your hand on the lad, or do anything to him; for I know that you fear God, since you have not withheld your son, your only son, from Me" (Genesis 22:12).

Because of what testing will do for us, we can be thankful for it. ""My brethren, count it all joy when you fall into various trials, knowing that the testing of your faith produces patience" (James 1:2-3).

"And not only that, but we also glory in tribulations,

knowing that tribulation produces perseverance; and perseverance, character; and character, hope" (Romans 5:3-4). Paul informs us we are saved by hope (Romans 8:24). Trials lead up to hope, so we ought to be thankful for testing or anything that will help us to be saved.

We do have the assurance that our burdens will not be too great. "No temptation has overtaken you except such as is common to man; but God is faithful, who will not allow you to be tempted beyond what you are able, but with the temptation will also make the way of escape, that you may be able to bear it" (1 Corinthians 10:13).

The other kind is temptation to do evil. This one does not come from God. James reveals the origin, nature and possible results of temptation.

"Blessed is the man who endures temptation; for when he has been approved, he will receive the crown of life which the Lord has promised to those who love Him. Let no one say when he is tempted, I am tempted by God; for God cannot be tempted by evil, nor does He Himself tempt anyone. But each one is tempted when he is drawn away by his own desires and enticed. Then when desire has conceived, it gives birth to sin; and sin when it is full-grown, brings forth death" (James 1:12-15).

Sin entered the world when Eve was deceived by Satan and ate of the forbidden tree. God had given clear instruction, because Eve was able to repeat what God had said when Satan asked her a question.

"And Adam was not deceived, but the woman being deceived, fell into transgression" (1 Timothy 2:14). The apostle Paul was afraid the Corinthians would fall like Eve, and warns them of it. "But I fear, lest somehow, as the serpent deceived Eve by his craftiness, so your minds may be corrupted from the simplicity that is in Christ" (2 Corinthians 11:3). It has ever been true that there is a battle for the minds of men. We are to love God with all our mind (Matthew 22:37).

The force of temptation is determined by the degree of desire created. The strength of our desire causes us to yield to temptation. Satan aims to destroy us (1 Peter 5:8), aand he uses deception to accomplish this. In fact, he is a liar and the father of it (John 8:44).

From the beginning, Satan has used the same method to defeat us. "For all that is in the world – the lust of the flesh, the lust of the eyes, and the pride of life – is not of the Father but is of the world" (1 John 2:16).

EVE WAS TEMPTED

Eve ate in order to become wise, which is the pride of life. She saw the fruit, which is the lust of the eyes. She saw it was good for food, which is the lust of the flesh. Satan told a lie, Eve heard, believed and obeyed a lie.

CHRIST WAS TEMPTED

Recorded in Matthew 4:1-12; Mark 1:12-13; Luke 4:1-13, Christ was tempted in all points as we are, yet without sin.

<u>Lust of the flesh.</u> After fasting for forty days and nights, Jesus was hungry. The devil said, "If you are the Son of God, command this stone to become read". Of course, He could have made bread out of the stones. He made the stones and could have changed them.

Our Lord used scripture to overcome temptation by quoting Deuteronomy 8:3, "Man shall not live by bread alone; but man lives by every word that proceeds from the mouth of the Lord."

<u>Pride of life.</u> Satan takes Him to the pinnacle of the temple, where the great deceiver quotes scripture to tell Him that He would cast Himself down that the angels would prevent any harm.

He quotes and misapplies Psalm 91:11-12. "For He shall give His angels charge over you, to keep you in all your ways.

In their hands they shall bear you up, Lest you dash your foot against a stone".

First, Satan uses the verse to say it was given with Christ in mind. There is no evidence this is true. The reply Christ gave was Deuteronomy 6:16, "You shall not tempt the Lord your God as you tempted Him in Massah." This does not mean one verse contradicts another, but one verse may give additional information, or modify what has been stated. We are told that Philip's daughters prophesied,(Acts 21:9), but this does not mean they were preachers, for 1 Timothy 2:11-12, modifies and restricts the role of women.

Second, It is certainly true, that God will protect us in time of danger, but it does not mean we are to be foolish and place ourselves in harms way to test God. Psalm 91 teaches the truth but Deuteronomy 6:16 modifies it.

LUST OF THE EYES

As the "god of this world" (2 Corinthians 4:3-4), Satan offers Him all the kingdoms of the world if He will fall down and worship Satan. Concerning the church, it was said that "all nations will flow unto it" (Isaiah 2:2-3), so to rule over all nations is why He came.

The reply to this temptation is Deuteronomy 6:13, "You shall fear the Lord your God and serve Him, and shall take oaths in His name." Our Savior resisted every temptation and "angels came and ministered to Him."

PURPOSES OF HIS TEMPTATIONS

1. To make Him the perfect sinless sacrifice (Hebrews 7:26-27).
2. To qualify Him to be our high priest (Hebrews 2:17).
3. To show us how to meet Satan. "It is written".

4. To show us He was human (Hebrews 2:14).
5. To destroy the works of Satan (1 John 3:8).

LESSONS WE CAN LEARN

If he tempted Christ, he will tempt us (Hebrews 4:15).
He strikes at the weakest point.
He can tempt in isolation. Wilderness or convent.
He seeks to plant doubts. "If you are the Son of God". He wants us to doubt God, Christ, Bible, one church, worship, morals.

WHAT CAN WE DO?

We must face temptation in same way Jesus did – with scripture (Matthew 4:4).
Pray about it (Matthew 6:13).
Associate with those who will influence us in the right way (1 Corinthians 15:33).
Regular worship (Hebrews 10:25).
Put on the whole armor of God (Ephesians 6:10-17).
One should become a Christian to enjoy the help God offers His people. This does not mean one will not be tempted, but by the grace of God and the help of fellow Christians one can be faithful.
"Yield not to temptation for yielding is sin."

Albert Gardner

CHAPTER 4 - SIN AND IT'S CONSEQUENCES

The logical place to begin is to define what sin is, for many do not know the true nature of sin. The prophet considered this a serious matter. "Woe to those who call evil good and good evil; who put darkness for light, and light for darkness; who put bitter for sweet, and sweet for bitter" (Isaiah 5:20)!

In the minds of so many, the whole value system is turned upside down. The reason for this is largely because they do not accept the correct standard by which to measure actions, so they do not get the right definition of sin. The Bible gives the exact definition of sin, and how to escape it. "Talk no more so very proudly; Let no arrogance come from your mouth, for the Lord is the God of knowledge; and by Him actions are weighed" (1 Samuel 2:3).

THE FIRST SIN

The instructions were simple, were understood, and Eve repeated them to the serpent. Satan told the first lie when he said, "you shall not die" (John 8:44). It is not a question of unclear instructions or lack of knowledge, but is a matter of belief. Eve believed a lie, and when God asked what she had done said, "The serpent deceived me, and I ate" (Genesis 3:13).

Disobedience, rejection of the authority of God, and deception are the basis of this sin. The results were fear, shame, separation from God and loss of fellowship with Him, and the sentence of physical death.

The long-range consequences are great. The serpent would crawl on the ground and eat of the dust. The woman would have pain in child bearing. Adam would have to make his living by the sweat of his face, for the ground would be cursed and in pain he would contend with thorns and thistles all the days of his life.

The first time sin is used in the Bible, is in connection with the sacrifice of Cain. "If you do well, will you not be accepted? And if you do not do well, sin lies at the door, and its desire is for you, but yoou should rule over it" (Genesis 4:7). In his case, he did not do well for he did not offer by faith (Hebrews 11:4).

The apostle John tells us what sin is. "Whoever commits sin also commits lawlessness, and sin is lawlessness" (1 John 3:4). This is an act of going against the law of God. James gives another meaning of sin by showing us that when we fail to do what is expected of us is sin. "Therefore, to him who knows to do good and does not do it, to him it is sin" (James 4:17). In either case it is an act by doing what is forbidden, or neglecting to do what is expected.

WHO IS GUILTY

"There is none righteous, no, not one" (Romans 3:10).

"For all have sinned and fall short of the glory of God" (Romans 3:23).

"If we say we have no sin, we deceive ourselves, and the truth is not in us" (1 John 1:8).

These verses answer the question well, without further

discussion or explanation.

ORIGINAL SIN

A very popular doctrine is the idea that babies are born with the guilt of Adam's sin, which is transferred biologically from parents to children. If a baby is guilty of sin, the practice of "baby baptism" is to take away sin, (Of course, they substitute sprinkling for the Bible requirement of immersion).

First, we cannot inherit sin because of what sin is. Sin is an act. It is the transgression of the law (1 John 3:4), or, it is a failure to do good that is expected of us (James 4:17). We cannot inherit what someone else does.

Second, we do not get our spirit from our parents. We get our bodies from our parents. That is the reason we may have black hair, blue eyes, dark complexion, and other family likenesses. But our spirit comes from God.

"Thus says the Lord, who stretches out the heavens, lays the foundation of the earth, and forms the spirit of man within him" (Zechariah 12:1).

Since God gives the spirit, if we have a sinful spirit, it would be God's fault. Why is sin universal? We did not start out that way. "They have all turned aside; they haave together become unprofitable; there is none who does good, no, not one" (Romans 3:12; Psalm 14:3). They were not born that way but they "turned aside", they "became " that way. The prodigal son was not born there but went to a foreign country. We are not born sinners but we become sinners.

Third, we do not inherit the quilt of Adam's sin, but we do suffer the consequences of his sin. A drunk driver may cause an accident, which may kill or injure several innocent people. They were not guilty but suffer the consequences of what another has done.

In the same way, we suffer the consequences of Adam's sin, rather than the guilt of his sin. One result of the first sin was physical death. Adam did not die a physical death immediately, but the sentence of death was upon him because he was driven from the Garden and away from the Tree of Life. "For as in Adam all die, even so in Christ all shall be made alive" (1 Corinthians 15:22). "Therefore, just as through one man sin entered the world, and death through sin, and thus death spread to all men, because all sinned" (Romans 5:12).

We will experience physical death as a consequence of the sin of Adam. "And as it is appointed for men to die once, but after this the judgment" (Hebrews 9:27).

PUNISHMENT FOR SIN

If one continues in sin and dies in that condition, his destiny is an eternal hell. It is death (Romans 6:23); John 5:28-29); weeping and gnashing of teeth (Matthew 8:12) torment (Luke 16:23-24); eternal darkness (Jude 6-7) everlasting (Matthew 25:46); separation from God (2 Thessalonians 1:7-9).

REMEDY FOR SIN

The Bible does not just point out that we are sinners but shows us the way to get rid of sin and how to be saved. When we could not help ourselves, Jesus came to save. "But God demonstrates His own love toward us, in that while we were still sinners, Christ died for us" (Romans 5:8).

There are great blessings of salvation during this life (Mark 10:30), along with the hope of eternal life (Mark 10:32; Titus 1:2). Then there is the great blessing of heaven where we will be with the Lord "which is far better" (Philippians 1:23). It is far better because we will be through with temptation and sin. There will be no more disappointments and hardships.

"And God will wipe away every tear from their eyes; there shall be no more death, nor sorrow, nor crying. There shall be

A Topical Study of Genesis

no more pain for the former things have passed away" (Revelation 21:4).

In the Bible sin is viewed in several ways: as an offense against God, which requires a pardon; as defilement, which requires cleansing; as slavery, which cries out for emancipation; as a debt, which must be canceled; as defeat, which must be reversed by victory; and as estrangement, which must be set right by reconciliation. However sin is viewed, it is thorough the work of Christ that the remedy is provided. He has procured the pardon, the cleansing, the emancipation, the cancellation, the victory, and the reconciliation." Nelson Bible Dictionary, page 670

Salvation Words. A study of words used for salvation are very interesting and revealing.

Justified. "Much more then, having now been justified by His blood, we shall be saved from wrath through Him" (Romans 5:9).

Reconciled . "For if when we were enemies we were reconciled to God through the death of His Son, much more, having been reconciled, we shall be saved by His life" (Romans 5:10).

Redeemed. We are redeemed "with the precious blood of Christ, as of a lamb without blemish and without spot" (1 Peter 1:19).

Forgiven. "In Him we have redemption through His blood, the forgiveness of sins, according to the riches of His grace" (Ephesians 1:7).

Sanctified. "Sanctify them by Your truth. Your word is truth" (John 17:17; 1 Corinthians 6:11).

Saved. "For by grace you have been saved through faith, and that not of yourselves; it is the gift of God (Ephesians 2:8).

Free from sin. "And having been set free from sin, you became slaves of righteousness" (Romans 6:18).

From a study of these passages we observe that salvation is made possible only by the blood of Christ. When one becomes a Christian, he is washed in the blood of the Lamb. "To Him who loved us and washed us from our sins in His own blood" (Revelation 1:5).

It is in baptism we reach His blood when we are baptized into His death (Romans 6:3), where He shed His blood (John 19:33-34). We are cleansed by His blood, which makes us new creatures (2 Corinthians 5:17), and are raised to walk a new life (Romans 6:4).

We will sin along the way and will stand in need of forgiveness by His blood. Constant cleansing is readily available for the Christian. "But if we walk in the light as He is in the light, we have fellowship with one another, and the blood of Jesus Christ His Son cleanses us from all sin" (1 John 1:7).

CHAPTER 5 - CAIN AND ABEL AND THEIR OFFERING

"Now Adam knew Eve his wife, and she conceived and bore Cain, and said, "I have acquired a man from the Lord."

Then she bore again, this time his brother Abel. Now Abel was a keeper of sheep, but Cain was a tiller of the ground.

And in the process of time it came to pass that Cain brought an offering of the fruit of the ground to the Lord.

Abel also brought of the firstborn of his flock and of their fat. And the Lord respected Abel and his offering, but He did not respect Cain and his offering. And Cain was very angry, and his countenance fell.

So the Lord said to Cain, "Why are you angry? And why has your countenance fallen?

"If you do well, will yoou not be accepted? And if you do not do well, sin lies at the door. And its desire is for you, but you should rule over it."

Now Cain talked with Abel his brother;; and it came to pass, when they were in the field, that Cain rose up against Abel his brother and killed him..

Then the Lord said to Cain, "Where is Abel your brother?" He said, "I do not know. Am I my brother's keeper?"

And He said, "What have you done? The voice of your brother's blood cries out to Me from the ground" (Genesis 4:1-10).

We learn from these verses: Abel was a keeper of sheep. He offered from the flock. God has respect to Abel and to his offering. Cain was a tiller of the ground. He offered of the fruit of the ground. God did not respect him or his offering. Cain became very angry and his countenance fell. God asked questions, not for His information, but to make Cain face the reality and guilt of his condition.

Why are you angry?

Why has your countenance fallen?

If you do well, will you not be accepted?

Where is Abel your brother?

What have you done?

Cain killed Abel, and when asked, "Where is Abel?", he lied and said "I do not know." The writer of Genesis writes as if the blood of Abel is a person. "The voice of your brother's blood cries out to Me from the ground" (Genesis 4:10).

Coffman lists the following things that the blood of Abel is saying:

The blood of Abel says that God will one day avenge the crimes perpetrated against the innocent (Romans 12:19).

The blood of Abel says that the righteous are hated without cause (1 John 3:11-13).

The blood of Abel says that it does make a difference how men worship Almighty God.

The blood of Abel says that faith is the only key to winning approval of God (Hebrews 11:6).

The blood of Abel says that the only righteousness is in obeying the word of the Lord (Romans 1:16,17). <u>Genesis 1, Burton Coffman commentaries.</u>

ADDITIONAL INFORMATION IN THE NEW TESTAMENT

It is stated God respected Abel AND his offering, and that He did not respect Cain AND his offering. Not only is the offering involved, but the one who offered was either accepted or rejected. What was this? The New Testament will shed some light on the character of these two brothers.

Matthew 23:35. "That on you may come all the righteous blood shed on the earth, from the blood of righteous Abel to the blood of Zechariah, son of Berechiah, whom you murdered between the temple and the altar."

Jesus calls him "righteous Abel". This is the reason the Lord had respect of Abel. He was godly, faithful and obedient. God will not hear the disobedient. "If I regard iniquity in my heart, the Lord will not hear" (Psalm 66:18). David tells the kind of heart God will accept. "The sacrifices of God are a broken spirit, a broken and a contrite heart – These, O God, You will not despise" (Psalm 51:17). David had experienced the very thing he writes about in Psalm 51. He recalls his concerning Uriah and Bathsheba. He can be forgiven because of repentance from a good heart.

1 John 3:11-12. "For this is the message that you heard from the beginning, that we should love one another, not as Cain who was of the wicked one and murdered his brother. And why did he murder him? Because his works were evil and his brother's righteous."

This verse helps us to understand why God did not accept Cain as well as his offering. He was following the wicked one. He became angry with God and his brother. He was jealous and envious of his brother because of the offering, and his heart was filled with hatred, which led to murder.

Isaiah shows the relation between the offering and the one who offers. "Bring no more futile sacrifices; incense is an abomination to Me. The New Moons, the Sabbaths, and the calling of assemblies – I cannot endure iniquity and the sacred meetings. Your New Moons and Your appointed feasts My soul hates; They are a trouble to Me, I am weary of bearing them. When you spread out your hands, I will hike My eyes from you; Even though you make many prayers, I will not hear. Yoour hands are full of blood: (Isaiah 1:13-15).

One cannot live one way and worship like life does not matter. "One who turns away his ear from hearing the law, even his prayer is an abomination" (Proverbs 28:9).

Hebrews 11:4. "By faith Abel offered to God a more excellent sacrifice than Cain, through which he obtained witness that he was righteous, God testifying of his gifts; and through it he being dead still speaks."

Abel offered by faith, and by this we know God gave instructions about the sacrifices, "So then faith comes by hearing, and hearing by the word of God" (Romans 10:17). When one does a thing by faith, he does it in obedience to the word of God. It is very simple, Abel offered by faith, and Cain didn't.

We do not know the details concerning instructions for their offering, but they had them and knew what would please God. Abel did it and Cain did not. That is the difference in Abel offering a more excellent sacrifice than Cain. Abel was righteous, and that made him and his offering acceptable.

It is stated that Abel "being dead still speaks". What is he saying about worship? What can we learn from him?

Abel is telling us if our worship is to be accepted, it must be done by faith.

He is saying our worship will not be accepted unless we are righteous.

He is saying we must worship in the way as directed by God.

He is saying there is penalty for disobeying.

Jude 11. "Woe to them! For they have gone in the way of Cain, have run greedily in the error of Balaam for profit, and perished in the rebellion of Korah."

The book of Jude has to do with false teachers that had slipped into the church unnoticed. They were ungodly men who had turned "the grace of our God into lewdness and deny the only Lord God and our Lord Jesus Christ" (Jude 4).

Among other things Jude says they have gone in the way of Cain. What had they done? What is the way of Cain.

The way of Cain was the way of a transgressor (Proverbs 14:12).

The way of Cain was the way of the evil one.

It was the way of jealousy, envy and hatred.

It was the way of a murderer (1 John 3:15).

It was the way of a liar (John 8:44).

It had little concern for the welfare of others.

It was the way of substitution.

OUR WORSHIP

Kinds of Worship. Vain (Matthew 15:8-9); ignorant (Acts 17:23); will (Colossians 2:20-23); true (John 4:23-24).

True worship has three major points.

IT MUST BE DIRECTED TO GOD.

- A. Not to idols (1 Corinthians 8:4-6).
- B. Not to men (Acts 10:25-26; 1 Corinthians 4:6).
- C. Not to angels (Revelation 22:8-9).

IT MUST BE IN RIGHT SPIRIT.

- A. In humility, reverence, and submission.
- B. With understanding.

IT MUST BE ACCORDING TO TRUTH.

A. F. Pilate asked, "What is truth?" (John 18:38).
B. G. Jesus gave the answer, "Sanctify them by Your truth. Your word is truth" (John 17:17).
C. H. This means what we do must be authorized in the New Testament.

CHAPTER 6 - SIN CAUSED THE FLOOD

"Now it came to pass, when men began to multiply on the face of the earth, and daughters were born to them that the sons of God saw the daughters of men, that they were beautiful; and they took wives for themselves of all whom they chose. And the Lord said, "My Spirit shall not strive with man forever, for he is indeed flesh; yet his days shall be one hundred and twenty years." There were giants on the earth in those days, and also afterward, when the sons of God came in to the daughters of men and they bore children to them. Those were the mighty men who were of old, men of renown. Then the Lord saw that the wickedness of man was great in the earth, and that every intent of the thoughts of his heart was only evil continually. And the Lord was sorry that He had made man on the earth, and He was grieved in His heart. So the Lord said, "I will destroy man whom I have created from the face of the earth, both man and beast, creeping thing and birds of the air, for I am sorry that I have made them." (Genesis 6:1-7)

It is not possible to determine the exact number of years or the population of the world at the time of the flood, but we know they had multiplied.

In The Genesis Flood, Whitcomb and Morris, pp 25-26; 396-398, calculate that between Adam and the flood (1600 years) the population of the world had increased geometrically to 774,000,000 by the time of the flood.

We do have records of world population in modern times, and by this we can observe population growth. It is estimated since Adam and Eve, population had doubled thirty times. In 1850 world population was one billion, and it took 80 years (1930) to be two billion. Only 30 years later (1960) it was three billion. On March 28,1976 (16 years) we had four billion. On July 7, 1986 (10 years) we reached five billion. On October 12, 1999 (13 years) we reached six billion.

Based on what we know of what is actually happening, the number given above of world population at the time of the flood seems reasonable.

There are two questions.

How did God's Spirit strive with man? What is the meaning of 120 years?

Did God strive or plead with the people directly? Or, did He do it through preaching? It was through Noah, "a preacher of righteousness" (2 Peter 2:5), that He tried to get people to repent. The preaching was done by Noah for 120 years while the ark was being prepared.

"For Christ also suffered once for sins, the just for the unjust, that He might bring us to God, being put to death in the flesh but made alive by the Spirit, by whom also He went and preached to the spirits in prison, who formerly were disobedient, when once the Divine longsuffering waited in the days of Noah, while the ark was being prepared, in which a few, that is, eight souls, were saved through water" (1 Peter 3:18-20).

These verses do not teach that after His death, Christ preached to the spirits of those who lived before the flood who did not repent. Notice 2 Peter 4:6. "For this reason the gospel was preached also to those who are dead, that they might be judged according to men in the flesh, but live according to God in the spirit." The preaching was done while they were living, but they are dead now.

It is by the Spirit through Noah that Christ preached to the people for 120 years, while the ark was being built. When something is done through another, it is the same as if they were doing it. It is said that Jesus made and baptized more disciples than John, though Jesus Himself did not baptize but His disciples" (John 4:1-2). Jesus baptized through His disciples. In the same way, Jesus preached to people before the flood through Noah. The doctrine that anyone will have an opportunity to repent after they die is in conflict with Bible teaching. We are to live right in this present world (Titus 2:11-12). We will be judged by what we have done in our body (2 Corinthians 5:10).

GOD REPENTED

In the New Testament when one repents, he changes his mind (Matthew 21:29). When God repents, what does He do? How can we harmonize "I do not change" (Malachi 3:6). It is said of God, "there is no variation or shadow of turning" (James 1:17). Christ is God, so we could expect the same from Him. "Jesus Christ is the same yesterday, today, and forever" (Hebrews 13:8).

"God is not a man, that He should lie, nor a son of man, that He should repent. Has He said, and will He not do? Or has He spoken, and will He not make it good?" (Numbers 23:19). Other verses clearly teach He did repent. There must be a difference between repentance which God does and repentance which man does. Men repent of sins, but God has no sins, but the idea of change certainly is taught.

Some translations do not use the word "repent", but instead use "relent" or "sorry". "And Jehovah repented of the evil which he said he would do unto his people" (Exodus 32:14 ASV). He "relented" NKJV. The idea of change is certainly in the words repent or relent.

When God saw the great wickedness of people, He was

grieved in His heart and repented or was sorry that He had made man. Halley says, "In respect to his essence, his attributes, his moral character, and his inflexible determination to punish sin and reward virtue. God is without "variableness or shadow of turning". Page 64.

It has been the plan of God all along to bless the obedient and punish the disobedient. When the faithful change to become unfaithful, God changes from blessing to punishment toward them. When Adam and Eve sinned, one punishment was, to be driven from Eden. Their relationship with God changed because they changed. When God saw the wickedness of the people, He said He would send the flood, but this was not that He just thought of punishment for the wicked and changed in that way. It had been His plan from the beginning.

God taught Jeremiah a lesson at the potter's house. A vessel marred in the hands of the potter, so he made it into another vessel as it seemed good to him. God says He can do for Israel in the same way.

"The instant I speak concerning a nation and concerning a kingdom, to pluck up, to pull down, and to destroy it, if that nation against whom I have spoken turns from its evil, I will relent of the disaster that I thought to bring upon it. And the instant I speak concerning a nation and concerning a kingdom, to build and to plant it, if it does evil in My sight so that it does not obey My voice, then I will relent concerning the good with which I said I would benefit it" (Jeremiah 18:7-10).

SONS OF GOD AND THE DAUGHTERS OF MEN

There is no need to take this to mean anything but that the sons of God were people who served and obeyed God, and the daughters of men did not serve and obey God.

It has been advanced by some, that the sons of God were angels and that they had children by the daughters of men. First, there is no indication that angels are meant since that is not the subject. Also, angels were never mentioned up to this time. Second, angels do not marry and reproduce for they are created beings.

The Sadducees (who do not believe in the resurrection) gave Jesus a supposed case of seven brothers. The first one married but died and left no children. According to the law, the next brother would take his wife and bear children in his name. All of them had her as a wife, but all of them died leaving no children. Their question was "In the resurrection, whose wife shall she be, since they all had her?"

Jesus answered, "You are mistaken, not knowing the scriptures nor the power of God. For in the resurrection they shall neither marry nor are given in marriage, but are like angels of God in heaven" (Matthew 22:24-30). Since angels do not marry, it is a false doctrine to say the sons of God are angels who had children by the daughters of men.

"And they took wives for themselves of all whom they chose." These are not condemned because they married, for God is the author of marriage, and it is approved in both testaments (Genesis 2:24; Hebrews 13:4). They were condemned because they chose the one they married based on their beauty or physical attraction. They gave no thought to character and spiritual relation to God. They were unconcerned about what they would teach the children who would be born, or whether they would hinder a pure relation with God.

Albert Gardner

CHAPTER 7 - THE FLOOD

A worldwide flood in the six hundredth year of Noah was real. It is not a myth. The mockers will reject the second coming of Christ and claim that things continue as they have from the beginning. Peter cites the flood to show things have not continued as they were from creation. They will say, "Where is the promise of His coming? For since the fathers fell asleep, all things continue as they were from the beginning of creation. For this they willfully forget: that by the word of God the heavens were of old, and the earth standing out of water and in the water, by which the world that then existed perished, being flooded with water" (2 Peter 3:4-6).

Both testaments affirm the reality of the flood. In connection with His second coming, Christ said, "But as the days of Noah were, so also will the coming of the Son of Man be. For as in the days before the flood, they were eating and drinking, marrying and giving in marriage, until the day that Noah entered the ark, and did not know until the flood came and took them all away so also will be the coming of the Son of Man "be" (Matthew 24:37-39). One who rejects the Genesis flood also rejects Christ who believed it.

In addition to inspired scripture, there is physical evidence over the world, which can be explained in no other way but by such a catastrophic event like the flood described in the Bible.

Albert Gardner

THE EARTH WAS CORRUPT AND VIOLENT

It is clear that sin was the cause of the flood, as a study of Genesis 6 will show. Sin was evidenced by their actions and their thoughts and it was wide spread. They chose women to marry based on physical beauty without regard to character and their relation to God. God looked into their hearts and saw they were wicked "and that every intent of the thoughts of his heart was evil continually" (Genesis 6:5). This lead to the moral decay of society. "The earth also was corrupt before God, and the earth was filled with violence. So God looked upon the earth, and indeed it was corrupt: for all flesh had corrupted their way on the earth" (Genesis 6:11-12).

It is also clear that the world stands today for at least two reasons. One, in order to give more people time to repent. "And consider that the longsuffering of our Lord is salvation" (2 Peter 3:15). His delay in returning is not a lack of purpose, but is for the benefit of sinners so they can repent (2 Peter 3:9).

Second, because of faithful and righteous people. When Abraham was informed Sodom would be destroyed because of great wickedness, Abraham asked if he could find fifty righteous people in the city would He spare the city. "So the Lord said, If I find in Sodom fifty righteous within the city, then I will spare all the place for their sakes" (Genesis 18:26).

Abraham brought the number down to ten, and God said He would save the city for ten righteous people. Because of wickedness and a lack of righteous people "the Lord rained brimstone and fire on Sodom and Gomorrah." (Proverbs 14:34; Proverbs 11:11; Romans 13:4).

UNIVERSAL – NOT LOCAL

A local flood does not fit all of the requirements given in the Bible. The moral purpose of the flood was to destroy all wicked and violent people (Genesis 6: 12-13). Though we don't know the exact population of the world at that time, we do know it was ten generations from Adam to Noah, so the population had grown and had no doubt scattered. A local flood would not have met the basic moral purpose of the flood, which was that all people would be destroyed except those saved in the ark.

This actually occurred for our Lord stated clearly what happened. "They ate, they drank, they married wives, they were given in marriage, until the day that Noah entered the ark, and the flood came and destroyed them all" (Luke 16:27). All of them were destroyed. Peter states that only eight souls were saved in the ark (1 Peter 3:20). This corresponds to the Genesis account (Genesis 7:13).

The ark was 300 cubits by 50 cubits by 30 cubits (6:15). A cubit was thought to be about eighteen inches, which would make the ark 450 feet by 75 feet by 45 feet. It should be noticed that the ark had three decks (6:16). It was a huge boat. If it were only a local flood, there would be no need for such a huge ark. In fact, for a local flood, there would be no need for an ark at all. Animals and people could go to higher ground and escape the flood.

WATER

It is difficult for us to grasp the great amount of water and the force of it during the flood. Even an isolated flash flood can sweep away people and even large objects such as houses and cars. One can only imagine what a flood would do that is twenty- two feet above the high hills (Genesis 7:20).

On the second day of creation, God formed the firmament. "Thus God made the firmament, and divided the waters which were under the firmament from the waters which were above the firmament; and it was so" (Genesis 1:7). It is important to know where God placed the water in the beginning, for this is the source of the water of the flood.

"In the six hundredth year of Noah's life, in the second month, the seventeenth day of the month, on that day all the fountains of the great deep were broken up, and the windows of heaven were opened" (Genesis 7:11). The water came from above and below.

The moral purpose of the flood was to destroy wickedness, sin and violence, which was accomplished. "And all flesh died that moved on the earth: birds and cattle and beasts and every creeping thing that creeps on the earth, and every man" (Genesis 7:21). Jesus said the flood "destroyed them all" (Luke 17:27). We are told that Noah, Shem, Ham, and Japheth and their wives entered the ark (Genesis 7:13), and only those with Noah in the ark remained alive (Genesis 7:23). Peter informs us that "eight souls were saved through water (1 Peter 3:20). God did what He said He would do.

It rained forty days and forty nights (Genesis 7:12). The flood waters increased and prevailed (Genesis 7:17-18), for one hundred and fifty days (Genesis 7:24). "And God made a wind to pass over the earth, and the waters subsided. The fountains of the deep and the windows of heaven were also stopped, and the rain from heaven restrained. And the waters receded continually from the earth. At the end of the hundred and fifty days the water decreased" (Genesis 8:1-3).

After coming out of the ark, Noah offered burnt offerings on an altar. God promised "Never again would there be such a flood to destroy every living creature (Genesis 8:21). "You have set a boundary that they may not pass over, that they may not return to cover the earth"(Psalm 104:9).

They were in the ark just over a year (Genesis 7:11; 8:14).

ARK

In order to save Noah and his family, and preserve the animals, God gave Noah a pattern for building an ark (Genesis 6:14-16). It was to be made of gopher wood, which is thought to be cyprus wood. It was to have rooms or compartments for different animals. It was to be covered inside and outside with pitch in order to make it waterproof.

The size of the ark was 300 cubits long, 50 cubits wide and 30 cubits high. It had three floors or decks, one window above and one door in the side. It has been a point of controversy as to whether the ark was large enough to accommodate all the animals. Two points need to be considered.

First, the size of the ark should be considered. A cubit was thought to be from the elbow to the tip of the middle finger. Obviously, that would vary from person to person. Most writers agree on a cubit being about eighteen inches. If that is accepted, the ark would be 450 feet long, 75 feet wide, and 45 feet high. Since there were three decks, each deck would have 33,750 square feet or a total of 101,250 square feet.

Second, the number and size of the animals should be considered. No details are given in the Bible about the selection of animals, so whatever is said is pure speculation. It would stand to reason that baby small animals would be taken.

It would not be necessary to take a pair of every animal in order to save a species. An Associated Press article tells about researchers studying 3, 241 dogs from 143 breeds of dogs using DNA and concluded dogs are descended from wolves. "Selective breeding has produced the many different types of dogs that exist today." Instead of taking a pair of 143 breeds of dogs, one pair of wolves would be sufficient. This would be true of horses, cows, and many animals.

We must not overlook the hand of God in all this, for this is something extraordinary. The animals came to Noah (Genesis 6:20). He did not go out to search and select them. God had a part in this. This was not a natural weather problem

Noah was dealing with, but a one time catastrophic event. Never before had it happened, and never again will anything like this occur.

Many details are left out, and many questions are unanswered, but the solution to all problems and questions surrounding the flood rests on our faith in God and His word. Noah built the ark to save himself and his family, and to save the animals. We believe he did exactly what God commanded.

CONTINENTAL DRIFT

There is the belief that at one time the continents were together, but over the years have drifted apart to their present state. This cannot be proved, and some writers think it is pure imagination.

By looking at the map it appears to fit, and this is one of the reasons for the claim. In 1912 Alfred Wegener and Frank Taylor presented the idea that there was one giant continent from which the "continents broke apart and drifted into their current locations. Wegener used the fit of the continents, the distribution of fossils, a similar sequence of rocks at numerous locations, ancient climates, and the apparent wandering of the Earth's polar regions to support his idea."

Since continental drift cannot be proved, and it is not necessary to believe it or disbelieve it, in order to accept what the Bible teaches about the flood, I do not care to discuss the theory further. This idea does involve what is referred to as "plate tectonics", and that deserves further study and research.

One problem about the flood would be solved if there was one continent, and that is the distribution of land animals after the flood. How could land animals get to Australia if it were not joined to land? One Bible verse is sometimes used to support Continental Drift in Genesis 10:25. "To Eber were born two sons: the name of one was Peleg, for in his days the earth was divided; and his brother's name was Joktan."

The context of this verse may be in connection with the

scattering of the people when their language was confused so they could not understand and they stopped building the Tower of Babel (Genesis 11:1-9). It may not refer to the land being divided but the people of the earth being scattered.

CHANGES BECAUSE OF THE FLOOD

That great changes were made by the flood is beyond question. Without dealing with the findings of Geology, it appears that there was climate change, for it is thought before the flood there was a world-wide warm climate. (Whitcomb and Morris, page 255)

It likely had not rained before the flood, for God had not caused it to rain and there was a mist that watered the ground (Genesis 2:5-6). Of course, this refers to a time before sin entered, but there is no evidence this was changed until Noah.

The crust of the earth, especially under the ocean has changed with mountains, earthquakes and volcanoes. "December 26,2004, an earthquake measuring 9.3, located 160 km off the western Coast of Sumatra, Indonesia, was the second largest earthquake ever recorded, that generated a massive tsunami which caused widespread damage on land and left 230,000 people dead in countries around the Indian ocean."

The strongest earthquake ever recorded was the Great Chilean Earthquake of May 22, 1960 with the magnitude of 9.5. About 6,000 people died.

"A tsunami is a series of waves created when a body of water, such as an ocean, is rapidly displaced on a massive scale. Earthquakes, mass movements, above or below the water, volcanic eruptions and other underwater explosions, landslides, large meteorite impacts and testing with nuclear weapons at sea, all have the potential to generate a tsunami." (Wikipedia Encyclopedea)

Atheists use human suffering as an argument against God. They claim that if He is a good God He would not allow storms and natural disasters that kill and injure people. We must address the question as to the cause of such events.

"But what of the suffering in today's world as a consequence of meteorological phenomena, such as hurricanes, earthquakes, etc. The first question to ask is: what produces the violent physical conditions of this planet? The answer is: the drastically different geophysical features of the globe, e.g., the mountain ranges, deserts, varying pressure areas, etc. But what created these divergent conditions, which precipitate the disasters to which we fall victim? Many scholars believe that the universal flood of Noah's day (Genesis 6-8) left behind the conditions which facilitate the occurrence of storms, earthquakes, etc. "<u>Bert Thompson FHU lecture, 1990, page 283.</u>

If this concept is true, how can we account for such things. It is certainly true that the flood was caused by sin, wickedness and violence on the earth (Genesis 6:5-12). At the flood, things were set in motion that would produce these things. Indirectly they were caused by sin, because sin caused the flood.

CHAPTER 8 - NOAH – A PREACHER OF RIGHTEOUSNESS

"And did not spare the ancient world, but saved Noah, one of the eight people, a preacher of righteousness, bringing in the flood on the world of the ungodly" (2 Peter 2:5).

In spite of the sin, violence, corruption and wickedness around him, it was possible for Noah to live right and try to get others to do right; As a preacher of righteousness, the only converts he had was his own family.

We have little information about what reaction the people had to his preaching other than complete rejection of it. Only Noah, his three sons and their wives were saved in the ark.

It is possible to live right in any situation, but we must first of all prepare our heart like David and Ezra (Daniel 1:8; Ezra 7:10). We must make up our minds to do right regardless what others say or do. It may not be easy. There may be opposition, mockery, abuse, mental or physical harm, but with determination to do right God will help us through.

The early church suffered many hardships and were faithful under persecution. The Jews in Rome came to hear Paul while he was under guard. "But we desire to hear from you what you think; for concerning this sect, we know that it is spoken against everywhere" (Acts 28:22).

"No temptation has overtaken you except such as is common to man; but God is faithful, who will not allow you to be tempted beyond what you are able, but with the temptation will also make the way of escape, that you may be able to bear it" (Romans 10:13).

"If any one speaks, let him speak as the oracles of God. If anyone ministers, let him do it as with the ability which God supplies, that in all things God may be glorified through Jesus Christ, to whom belong the glory and the dominion forever and ever. Amen" (1 Peter 4:11).

In regard to persecution, Paul asks a very important question with an obvious answer, "If God is for us, who can be against us?" (Romans 8:31).

The first century Christians faced physical harm and abuse, even to the taking or destroying of personal property. The writer of Hebrews gives words of encouragement and hope as they face trials. "But recall the former days in which, after you were illuminated, you endured a great struggle with sufferings: partly while you were made a spectacle both by reproaches and tribulations, and partly while you became companions of those who were so treated; for you had compassion on me in my chains, and joyfully accepted the plundering of your goods, knowing that you have a better and an enduring possession for yourselves in heaven. Therefore do not cast away your confidence, which has great reward. For you have need of endurance, so that after you have done the will of God, you may receive the promise" (Hebrews 10:32-36).

The spoiling of their goods was endured joyfully, because they were not so attached to this world, which will perish, but instead, had their eye on that "inheritance incorruptible and undefiled and that does not fade away, reserved in heaven for you" (1 Peter 1:4). There is a great lesson in this for all of us. God has promised help during trials.

SAVED LIKE NOAH

The salvation of Noah is a type of our salvation (1 Peter 3:20-21).

New Testament verses show a belief in the reality of the flood, and it is not a myth or a folk tale. Jesus mentioned it in connection with His second coming (Matthew 24:37-39). Noah and the ark are mentioned in Hebrews 11:7.

The apostle Peter says that our salvation is, in some respects, is like the salvation of Noah. "There is also an antitype which now saves us – baptism (not the removal of the filth of the flesh, but the answer of a good conscience toward God), through the resurrection of Jesus Christ (1 Peter 3:20 – 21).

The Bible uses types and antitypes to teach some great lessons. It is like a prophecy of some future event.

John 3:14-15. "And as Moses lifted up the serpent in the wilderness, even so must the Son of Man be lifted up, that whoever believes in Him should not perish but have eternal life." In Numbers 21:6-9, because the people spoke against God and Moses, God sent fiery serpents that bit many people and they died. The people came to Moses and confessed their sins, so God told Moses to make a brazen serpent and put it on a pole, and anyone who was bitten if they looked on it they lived. In the save way those in sin who look with faith on Jesus on the cross will be saved.

1 PETER 1:18-20 The sacrifice of a lamb under the priesthood of Levi in the Old Testament is like the sacrifice of Christ who is called the Lamb of God (John 1:29; Revelation 5:6). The lamb offered was not to be sick or crippled, so we are redeemed "with the precious blood of Christ, as of a lamb without blemish and without spot" (1 Peter 1:19). Every lamb offered under the law pointed to the perfect Lamb – Christ, "who committed no sin, nor was deceit found in His mouth" (1 Peter 2:22).

In 1 Peter 3:20-21, quoted above, we see the type and antitype. We are familiar with a rubber stamp, which is the type. What it prints is the antitype. Whatever is on the rubber stamp, it will print. It will not print something different.

When the Passover lamb was killed not a bone was to be broken (Numbers 9:12; Exodus 12:46). That is the type, so the antitype will be like it. When Roman soldiers came to break the legs of those on the crosses, they did not break His legs (John 19:33). This fulfilled the Scripture "not one of His bones shall be broken" (John 19:36).

In what ways is the salvation of Noah like our salvation? There are at least four things involved in the salvation of Noah that are also required for our salvation.

NOAH WAS SAVED BY GRACE

"But Noah found grace in the eyes of the Lord" (Genesis 6:8). He is said to be "perfect in his generation. Noah walked with God" (Genesis 6:9). God said he was righteous (Genesis 7:1).

A simple definition of grace is unmerited favor. If anyone is ever saved from sin it will be by grace. The reason Noah found favor with God is that he walked with God.

We can never do enough good works, pray enough, or give enough to deserve salvation. Jesus made it clear. "So likewise you, when you have done all those things which you are commanded, say, we are unprofitable servants. We have done what was our duty to do" (Luke17:10).

"Now to him who works, the wages are not counted as grace but as debt" (Romans 4:4). When one is employed by another, he receives wages. He owes you wages for your work. You deserve it, so it is not grace. Grace is something that is unmerited.

"Not by works of righteousness which we have done, but according to His mercy He saved us, through the washing of regeneration and renewing of the Holy Spirit" (Titus 3:5).

A Topical Study of Genesis

"For by grace you have been saved through faith, and that not of yourselves; it is the gift of God, not of works, lest anyone should boast" (Ephesians 2:8-9).

There is not a conflict between Ephesians 2:8-9, (which says we are not saved by works), and James 2:24 (which says we are justified by works). James refers to works of obedience and gives Abraham as an example. God commanded and he obeyed. Paul wrote of works about which we could boast. We are not saved by that kind of works. There are two kinds of works, we are saved by one but not the other.

Though we are saved by grace, it will not remove our part in our own salvation. Ephesians 2:8 says we are saved by grace (God's part) through faith (man's part). This is the way we accept grace.

Grace will not eliminate repentance. "But where sin abounded, grace abounded much more" (Romans 5:20). Where sin is great, grace will be great to take care of it. In view of this the apostle Paul raises this question about it. "What shall we say then?? Shall we continue in sin that grace may abound? Certainly not! How shall we who died to sin live any longer in it" (Romans 6:1-2).

In other words, shall we keep sinning so we will have more grace? The answer is certainly not. When we become Christians we repent of our sins, and that involves a change of mind about sin, which leads to stopping sin. If we are dead to sin, how can we continue in it?

In 1 Corinthians 6:9-11 we see a list of sins, and Paul says about the Christians at Corinth "and such were some of you, but you were justified in the name of the Lord Jesus and by the Spirit of our God."

Some of them were fornicators, homosexuals, thieves, drunkards, etc., that is they "were" guilty of these sins but not now. You were but you were washed in baptism, sanctified and justified. Repentance means they quit these sins. Paul taught that when we become Christians we put off the old man, and put on the new man in righteousness (Ephesians 4:22-24).

As Paul was ready to leave a the brethren at Ephesus, he

admonishes them to remain faithful. "So now, brethren, I commend you to God and to the word of His grace, which is able to build you up and give you an inheritance among all those who are sanctified" (Acts 20:32). Notice it is the "word" of His grace. God extends grace to us through His word.

After the conversion of Cornelius, there was rejoicing because they realized that "God has also granted to the Gentiles repentance to life" (Acts 11:18). Up to this time, there was preaching only to Jews, but certain ones came to Antioch and preached to the Hellenists (these were Greek speaking Jews). "And the hand of the Lord was with them and a great number believed and turned to the Lord" (Acts 11:21).

When news about this reached Jerusalem, the church sent Barnabas to Antioch. "When he came and had seen the grace of God, he was glad, and encouraged them all that with purpose of heart they should continue with the Lord" (Acts 11:23). Barnabas saw the grace of God. What did he see? He saw people who had heard the preaching of the Lord Jesus, who believed it and turned to the Lord. When people hear, believe and obey the gospel, they are saved by grace.

When the Ethiopian eunuch heard Philip preach Christ, he believed it, confessed his faith, was baptized and went on his way rejoicing (Acts 8:26-40). He had been saved by grace, which was the reason for rejoicing.

The Corinthians heard, believed and were baptized (Acts 18:8). They were saved by grace. Enoch walked with God (Genesis 5:24) "for before he was taken he had this testimony, that he pleased God" (Hebrews 11:5). Amon "forsook the Lord God of his fathers, and did not walk in the way of the Lord" (2 Kings 21:22). Josiah "did what was right in the sight of the Lord, and walked in all the ways of his father David; he did not turn aside to the right hand or to the left" (2 Kings 22:2). Jehoshaphat "sought the God of his father, and walked in His commandments and not according to the act of Israel" (2 Chronicles 17:4). Jeremiah said of some, "they have not walked in My law or in My statutes that I set before you and your fathers (Jeremiah 44:10).

Over and over we learn of punishment for those who did not walk according to the commands of God. To walk with God, means we obey Him. That is what Noah did.

NOAH WAS SAVED BY ODEDIENCE

"Thus Noah did according to all that God commanded him, so he did" (Genesis 6:22).

The reason he was saved by grace was the fact that he walked with God (Genesis 6:8). What does it mean to walk with God? Is there a way to know if we are walking with God?

Just as Noah was saved by obedience, we are also saved by obedience. Jesus set the example for us. "For I have come down from heaven, not to do My own will, but the will of Him who sent Me" (John 6:38).

"Though He was a Son, yet He learned obedience by the things which He suffered. And having been perfected, He became the author of eternal salvation to all who obey Him" (Hebrews 5:8-9).

"Not everyone who says to Me, Lord, Lord, shall enter the kingdom of heaven, but he who does the will of My Father in heaven" (Matthew 7:21).

When the people on Pentecost asked what to do to be saved, they were told to repent and be baptized for the remission of sins (Acts 2:37-38).

NOAH WAS SAVED BY FAITH

"By faith Noah, being divinely warned of things not yet seen, moved with godly fear, prepared an ark for the saving of his household, by which he condemned the world and became heir of the righteousness which is according to faith" (Hebrews 11:7).

God gave instructions to Noah for building the ark, and

how He would save Noah and his family along with the animals (Genesis 6:14-22). He did all that God commanded him. It is said that he prepared the ark by faith. What does it mean to do a thing by faith? How does faith come? We need the proper answers to these questions because we are saved like Noah. He was saved by faith and so will we be saved that way.

"So then faith comes by hearing and hearing by the word of God" (Romans 10:17). That means whatever we teach and practice must be authorized by the word of God. When God commands and we do it, it is an act of faith. Jesus told the woman at the well about true worship. "God is Spirit, and those who worship Him must worship in spirit and truth" (John 4:24). Instrumental music cannot be done by faith because it is not authorized in the New Testament. There is no command for it, and no example of it to follow, and there is no necessary inference for it.

We eat the Lord's Supper each first day of the week because the Lord instructed us to do it, and we have an example to follow (Acts 20:7). We do it as an act of faith.

Hebrews 11 gives several examples that show what it means to walk by faith. We mention some of them, with the hope you will study them more deeply.

Cain and Abel. "By faith Abel offered to God a more excellent sacrifice than Cain, through which he obtained witness that he was righteous, God testifying of his gifts; and through it he being dead still speaks" (Hebrews 11:4).

Other information is given in Genesis 4:4-5 concerning the sacrifices of these two brothers. "And the Lord respected Abel and his offering, but He did not respect Cain and his offering." What is the difference? Since Abel offered by faith, it means God had given instructions about the sacrifices. One obeyed and the other one did not. Abel offered by faith and Cain did not.

Abraham. In Genesis 12:1-3, God called Abraham to leave his country and go to a land He would show him. Notice what happened. "By faith Abraham obeyed when he was called to go out to the place which he would receive for an inheritance. He went out, not knowing where he was going" (Hebrews 11:8). God spoke and he did it. He obeyed by faith because faith comes by hearing God's word.

Walls of Jericho. "By faith the walls of Jericho fell down after they were encircled for seven days" (Hebrews 11:30). In Joshua 6 we read of the instructions God gave for taking the city. Their marching around the city was an act of faith, and the walls fell down.

Our Salvation. Like Noah we are saved by faith. "But without faith it is impossible to please Him, for he who comes to God must believe that He is, and that He is a rewarder of those who diligently seek Him" (Hebrews 11:6). Many verses teach we are to have faith.

What we are to do to be saved must come from the New Testament, for that is the way faith comes. One could not practice sprinkling because one cannot read about it in the New Testament. When one is buried in baptism, it is an act of faith (Romans 6:4-5).

In Acts 2:37-41, they asked what to do, and were told to repent and be baptized. Luke informs us that about three thousand gladly received the word and were baptized. What they did was an act of faith because Peter spoke the word of God. That is the way Noah was saved. God spoke and he obeyed.

NOAH WAS SAVED BY WATER

"Eight souls were saved through water". When the "fountains of the great deep were broken up and the windows of heaven were opened. The waters prevailed fifteen cubits (22 feet) upward, and the mountains were covered" (Genesis 7:11, 20). The ark floated on the water and in this way Noah, his three sons and their wives were saved by water.

That example is a type, and our salvation is the antitype. "There is also an antitype which now saves us – baptism (not the removal of the filth of the flesh, but the answer of a good conscience toward God), through the resurrection of Jesus Christ" (1 Peter 3:21). Just as Noah was saved by water, so we are saved by baptism.

Some reject the teaching that baptism saves, but it is clearly stated in this verse as well as other verses (Mark 16:16; Acts 2:38; 22:16). Baptism saves but the power is not in the water but the cleansing power is in the blood of Christ.

Jesus shed His blood in His death. The Roman soldiers came to break His legs but He was already dead, so they pierced His side and from His side came blood and water (John 19:33-34). If we are to benefit from His blood, we must reach His blood. It is in baptism we reach His death where He poured out His blood for our sins.

There is physical circumcision, which is a surgical operation. There is also spiritual circumcision that takes place in baptism. "In Him you were also circumcised with the circumcision made without hands, by putting off the body of sins of the flesh, by the circumcision of Christ, buried with Him in baptism in which you also were raised with Him through faith in the working of God, who raised Him from the dead" (Colossians 2:11-12).

What happens in spiritual circumcision is that we are buried in baptism into the death of Christ, where we contact His blood. It is then that the operation of God takes place and our sins are taken away by the blood of Christ. That is how we are raised to walk in newness of life, for we are new creatures in Christ (Romans 6:4; 2 Corinthians 5:17).

There is no power in water to forgive sins, but there is power in the blood. The way baptism saves is that it puts us in touch with the saving blood. Peter was not teaching water salvation, for he knew we are redeemed by the blood of the Lamb (1 Peter 1:18-20).

One who refuses baptism, is refusing salvation by the blood of Christ.

Our salvation is like Noah's salvation. Grace, obedience, faith and water baptism are essentials in our salvation.

CHAPTER 9 - ABRAHAM A FRIEND OF GOD

Abraham came from a family who worshiped idols (Joshua 24:2). It takes courage and deep convictions to turn from idols to serve the living God. Paul preached and the people at Thessalonica did that very thing (1 Thessalonians 1:9). Only the gospel is powerful enough to cause people to leave idols, turn to Christ in genuine faith and obedience, with the promise of salvation from sin.

Idols do not offer help or hope. Notice the contrast between God and idols. "Not unto us, o Lord, not unto us, but to Your name give glory, because of Your mercy, because of Your truth. Why should the Gentiles say, So where is their God?" But our God is in heaven; He does whatever He pleases. Their idols are silver and gold, the work of men's hands. They have mouths, but they do not speak; Eyes they have, but they do not see; They have ears, but they do not hear; Noses they have, but they do not smell; They have hands, but they do not handle; Feet they have, but they do not walk; Nor do they mutter through their throat. Those who make them are like them; so is everyone who trusts in them. O Israel, trust in the Lord; He is their help and their shield." (Psalms

115:1-9)

Isaiah 44:13-17, the prophet shows how weak and helpless idols are. He says one will cut down a tree, with part of it he will warm himself, with part of it he will cook his food, and with part of it he makes a carved image, and "falls down before it and worships it, prays to it and says deliver me for you are my god." It is useless to expect help from such a god. Paul spoke of God in Athens. "Nor is He worshiped with men's hands, as though He needed anything, since He gives to all life, breath, and all things" (Acts 17:25).

CALL OF ABRAHAM

Abram (before his name was changed to Abraham (Genesis 17:5), was told to leave his country and his family, and go to a land God would show him. He was seventy-five years old when he went to Haran. God gave three promises which were fulfilled in due time. These included land, nation and seed (Genesis 12:1-3).

Land promise. When Israel came from Egypt, the land was divided among the tribes under the leadership of Joshua. "So the Lord gave to Israel all the land of which He had sworn to give to their fathers, and they took possession of it and dwelt in it" (Joshua 21:43).

Nation promise. A census was taken when the people came from Egypt, and the number was six hundred three thousand five hundred and fifty. Women, children and the entire tribe of Levi were not included in this number. Only men who were twenty years old and above and were able to go to war were counted (Numbers 2:32-33); 1:3).

Seed promise. These promises were restated to Isaac (Genesis 26:2-4), and to Jacob (Genesis 28:13-14). The apostle Paul also recalls these promises and explains the see promise. "Now to Abraham and his Seed were the promises made. He does not say, and to seeds, as of many, but as of one, and to your Seed, who is Christ" (Galatians 3:16).

The seed promise was fulfilled in Christ. The way we are blessed is to be in Christ and belong to Him. "And if you are Christ's, then you are Abraham's seed, and heirs according to the promise" (Galatians 3:29). The way we get into Christ is through baptism (Galatians 3:27).

At the time the promise was given Abraham and Sarah had no children. Though Abraham never doubted (Romans 4:20-21), he just did not know how it would be done. He asked God to let Eliezer be the one through whom the seed would come. He was told it would be his own son (Genesis 15:2-6).

Sarah gave her maidservant, Hagar, to Abraham and he could have children by her. Ishmael was born when Abraham was eighty six (Genesis 16).

God appears to Abraham when he was ninety nine, restates the former promises, and tells him Isaac will be born to Sarah. Abraham asked that Ishmael would be the one throough whom the Seed would be called. God said Ishmael would beget twelve princes and he would be a great nation. "But My covenant I will establish with Isaac, whom Sarah shall bear to you at this set time next year" (Genesis 17:21). Muslims want to count through Ishmael, but it is clearly stated it will be through Isaac and not Ishmael.

ABRAHAM IS TESTED

After Isaac was born and Abraham knew he was the child of promise through whom the seed promise would be fulfilled, God puts him to a severe test.

"Then He said, Take now your son, your only son Isaac, whom you love, and go to the land of Moriah, and offer him there as a burnt offering on one of the mountains of which I shall tell you" (Genesis 22:2).

This was an act of faith. "By faith Abraham, when he was tested, offered up Isaac, and he who had received the promises offered up his only begotten son (Hebrews 11:17). This is also an act of works. "Was not Abraham our father justified by works when he offered Isaac his son on the altar?" (James 2:21). When we are obedient to the command of God, it is works of obedience and an act of faith.

In this incident we can also see the difference between faith, opinion and knowledge. Faith was when Abraham concluded God would raise Isaac from the dead, though He had said nothing about it (Hebrews 11:19). Knowledge was when he saw the ram whose horns were caught in a thicket (Genesis 22:13).

Another lesson we can learn is the difference between general and specific commands. God gave a specific command to offer Isaac. It would have been wrong for him to offer any other family member. When a specific command is given, it excludes all else. The command is to sing in worship and make melody in the heart. That is specific to sing, and that excludes playing. When a general command is given we are free to choose. Jesus said go preach the gospel, but he did not say how to go. We can ride a camel, bus, airplane, walk, or run. We can choose. If he had given a specific command to "go by camel", we would be limited to that one way though other means are available.

ABRAHAM WAS A MAN OF FAITH

We have his example in the Old Testament, and his faitih is often mentioned in the New Testament. Anything that is taught in both testaments can be studied in both. Faith, obedience and faithfulness are taught in both testaments. Sabbath keeping, instrumental music in worship and offering burnt offerings are not a part of New Testament worship, so they may be studied only from the Old Testament.

When God asked Abraham to count the stars, and He said this is the way his descendents would be. "And he believed in the Lord, and He accounted it to him for righteousness" (Genesis 15:6). God is the One who determines righteousness. Abraham believed and God said that is equal to righteousness.

Faith is not just mental consent, but is active to obey. "By faith Abraham obeyed when he was called to go out to the place which he would receive as an inheritance. And he went out not knowing where he was going" (Hebrews 11:8).

Jesus explains the Parable of the Sower, and says the rocky soil aree those "who believe for a while and in time of temptation fall away" (Luke 8:13). Thayer defines the word for believe as "conjoin with obedience." That is the kind of faith Abraham has as demonstrated by his life.

ABRAHAM FEARED GOD

The angel of the Lord saved Isaac when He said to Abraham "Do not lay your hand on the lad, or do anything to him; for now I know that you fear God, since you have not withheld your son, your only son, from me" (Genesis 22:12).

He was not afraid of God in the sense we would be afraid of some danger. Vine defines it as "reverential fear of God, as a controlling motive of the life, in matters spiritual and moral, not a mere fear of His power and righteous retribution but a wholesome dread of displeasing Him, a fear which banishes the terror that shrinks from His presence."

Solomon says this is involved in oour whole duty. "Let us hear the conclusion of the whole matter: Fear God and keep His commandments, for this is man's all" (Ecclesiastes 12:13).

ABRAHAM WORSHIPED GOD

Where Abraham pitched his tent, he built an altar. God appeared to him in Shechem and he built an altar (Genesis 12:7). He moved to Bethel, pitched his tent and built an altar (Genesis 12:8). He moved his tent to Mamre and built an altar to the Lord (Genesis 13:4, 18).

His response of thanksgiving in worship was based on the

blessings of God and the promises he had given. We have so many spiritual blessings, including the forgiveness of sins, which should cause us never to forsake worship.

HE WAS A PEACEMAKER

There arose strife between the herdsmen of Abraham and Lot because the grazing land was not able to support them. "So Abraham said to Lot, please let there be no strife between you and me, and between my herdsmen and your herdsmen; for we are brethren" (Genesis 13:8).

Abraham gave Lot the choice of all the land. If Lot went one direction, he would go the other way. Lot pitched his tent toward Sodom because of the well watered plain of the Jordan. This proved to be a bad decision.

Jesus taught us to be peacemakers. "Blessed are the peacemakers, for they shall be called sons of God" (Matthew 5:9).

HE WAS A GOOD FATHER

"For I have known Him, in order that he may command his children and his household after him, that they keep the way of the Lord, to do righteousness and justice, that the Lord may bring to Abraham what He has spoken to him" (Genesis 18:19).

There is such a great need in our world for fathers to follow the example of Abraham. Fathers need to be the spiritual leaders of their families. They need to set the right example, but they also need to command, teach and guide their children. Their failure to do so has caused some wives to take leadership in the home, which is contrary to the plan God had for the home.

God put the husband as head in the family(Ephesians 5:23).

Fathers are directed to bring up their children in the right way. The wife and mother has a duty in this but the father is to take the lead. (Ephesians 6:4; Colossians 3:21).

Fathers may do the very best they can in teaching and example, and sometimes children still go astray. All of the fault does not belong to fathers in every case. Adam sinned though he had a perfect Father. He had freedom to choose and he made the wrong choice. God was not at fault in any way. Our children come to the point when they make all decisions about their lives, and they do not always choose to do right. When that happens, parents are not at fault.

This may in part, explain why some good parents have bad children. Eli failed with his sons because he restrained them not (1 Samuel 3:13), but he seems to have had a good influence on Samuel. Though Samuel was a faithful judge, "his sons did not walk in his ways; they turned aside after dishonest gain, took bribes, and perverted justice" (1 Samuel 8:3). David was a man after God's own heart, but his son Absalom tried to overthrow his father's government and become king in his place.

Jewish parents were to diligently teach their children the law of God and train them in the way they should go (Deuteronomy 6:4-9; Proverbs 22:6). Christians would do well to follow that example.

ABRAHAM WAS INTERESTED IN THE WELFARE OF OTHERS

When Lot was captured, Abraham armed three hundred and eighteen trained servants and went in pursuit and rescued Lot his household and his goods (Genesis 14:11-16).

Three angels appeared to Abraham and he ran to meet them. He insisted that he wash their feet, prepare food for them so they might rest and refresh themselves. These angels later informed him about the coming destruction of Sodom.

He tried to save the city by searching for as many as ten righteous people.

ABRAHAM MET MELCHIZEDEK

After the rescue of Lot, Abraham met Melchizedek, and two significant things happened. Melchizedek blessed Abraham, and Abraham gave a tithe to Melchizedek (Genesis 14:18-24). In the book of Hebrews, the meeting of Melchizedek and Abraham is discussed, to show that Christ is a priest like Melchizedek, and that that His priesthood is greater than the priesthood of Levi and Aaron.

First, "beyond all contradiction the lesser is blessed by the better: (Hebrews 7:7). Since Melchizedek blessed Abraham, it means Melchizedek is greater than Abraham. Since Levi would come from Abraham, it would mean the priesthood of Melchizedek is greater than the priesthood of Levi.

Second, Abraham paid tithes to Melchizedek, which shows Melchizedek is greater than Abraham (Hebrews 7:4). It also means the priesthood of Melchizedek is greater than the priesthood of Levi that would later come through Abraham.

Melchizedek was "without father, without mother, without genealogy, having neither beginning of days nor end of life, but made like the Son of God, remains a priest continually" (Hebrews 7:3). This does not refer to Melchizadek as a person but to his priesthood. Unlike the priesthood of Levi who could trace their lineage from Aaron the first high priest, Melchizedek had no one in his family before him or after him who were priests. In this way Christ is a priest after the order of Melchizedek, for He had no one in His family (Judah) who were priests (Hebrews 7:12-14). Christ has an unchangeable priesthood (Hebrews 7:24).

CONCLUSION

"Are You not our God, who drove out the inhabitants of

this land before Your people Israel, and gave it to the descendants of Abraham Your friend forever?" (2 Chronicles 20:7).

"And the scripture was fulfilled which says, Abraham believed God, and it was accounted to him for righteousness. And he was called a friend of God" (James 2:23).

"You are my friends if you do whatever I command you" (John 15:14).

"No man can serve two masters; for either he will hate the one and love the other, or else he will be loyal to the one and despise the other. You cannot serve God and mammon" (Matthew 6:24).

Albert Gardner

CHAPTER 10 - LOT GOES TO SODOM

Lot is mentioned in the genealogy of Shem (Genesis 11:27). Lot's father, Haran, died in Ur. Terah, father of Abraham, took Abraham, Sarah and Lot to Haran. Abram, whose name was changed to Abraham, was called of God to leave his country and his family, and go to a land God would show him and which he would inherit. His nephew, Lot, went with him to the land of Canaan. Though Terah worshiped idols (Joshua 24:2), Abraham served the true God.

LOT'S BAD CHOICE

Both Abraham and Lot had accumulated great wealth measured by their flocks and herds. Because their possessions were so great, the grazing land could not support them, so there was strife between the herdsmen of Abraham and the herdsmen of Lot.

Abraham gave the solution for peace. "Is not the whole land before you? Please separate from me. If you take the left, then I will go to the right; or, if you go to the right, then I will go to the left" (Genesis 13:9).

When Lot saw the well watered plain of Jordan, he chose it,

and pitched his tent toward Sodom. His decision was based on what he could see, and had to do with material things without regard to where that choice would lead him in spiritual matters. We know as we read about his life, it was a decision that caused the loss of his wealth, but especially, he lost his wife and children and led to incest with his two daughters.

When we make choices based on money or worldly gain, usually it is a bad decision. Spiritual matters such as personal responsibility to God, the welfare of the wife and children, should be considered. An advancement in a job sometimes takes one away from the church and the good influence of godly people which may weaken the family.

The example of Moses and his choice teaches a far different lesson. "By faith Moses, when he became of age, refused to be called the son of Pharaoh's daughter, choosing rather to suffer affliction with the people of God than to enjoy the passing pleasures of sin, esteeming the reproach of Christ greater riches than the treasures in Egypt; for he looked to the reward" (Hebrews 11:24-26).

If we look at the immediate surroundings, like Lot did, Moses was foolish to give up the wealth, power and maybe even the throne in Egypt. Moses did not decide to become identified with a people in slavery and their suffering based on what he could see, but on the long term and the reward. That is the way we should make decisions.

ABRAHAM TRYS TO SAVE SODOM

Sodom had "given themselves over to sexual immorality and gone after strange flesh, are set forth as an example, suffering the vengeance of eternal fire" (Jude 7). They were homosexuals, and this practice had affected the entire population of the city. They were "old and young, all the people from every quarter" (Genesis 19:4).

God called it a very grave sin (Genesis 18:20), which would bring about the total destruction of the city and all the inhabitants, as well as what grew on the ground (Genesis 19:25). None would escape. All would be destroyed. If God destroyed Sodom for this sin, why do people today think they can make homosexuality respectable and have the approval of God? (Romans 1:24-27). They need to learn the truth of Proverbs 14:34, "Righteousness exalts a nation, but sin is a reproach to any people". Abraham and Lot called it wickedness. It is not just another lifestyle. It is sin (Genesis 18:23; 19:7).

When God informed Abraham that He would destroy Sodom because of their sin, Abraham asked, "Would you also destroy the righteous with the wicked?" (Genesis 18:23). He asked the Lord if he could find fifty righteous people in the city, would He spare the city? God agreed to spare the city if Abraham could find fifty righteous people. He reduces the number to forty-five, forty, thirty, twenty and finally ten. God agreed to spare Sodom for righteous people, but Abraham could not find even ten.

The world stands and the Lord delays His coming because of righteous people on the earth. The flood destroyed all the people on the earth, except eight, because of sin, wickedness and violence. God still honors and blesses people and nations for righteousness.

REMEMBER LOT'S WIFE

Two angels were sent to Sodom to inform Lot and to destroy Sodom and Gomorrah and the cities around them. They asked Lot if he had son-in-law, sons and daughters in the city, and warned him to take them out of the city. "So Lot went out and spoke to his sons-in-law, who had married his daughters, and said, Get up, get out of this place; for the Lord will destroy this city! But to his sons-in-law he seemed to be joking" (Genesis 19:14).

The angels took them by the hand and tried to rush them to leave the city, and told them not to look back. "But his wife looked back behind him, and she became a pillar of salt" (Genesis 19:26).

Jesus used their example to teach how it would be when He returns. "Likewise as it was also in the days of Lot: They ate, they drank; they bought, they sold, they planted, they built; but on the day that Lot went out of Sodom it rained fire and brimstone from heaven and destroyed them all. Even so will it be in the day when the Son of Man is revealed" (Luke 17:28-30).

As a reminder of the punishment of sin, Jesus said, "Remember Lot's wife" (Luke 17:32). Not much is said about her. Her name is not stated. The reason she looked back is not revealed. We do know that she was told the city would be destroyed, and she was to leave the city. We know she hesitated and lingered. We know the angels took Lot, his wife and their two daughters by the hand in order to speed up their departure from the doomed city. They were told not to look back. We also know that Lot's wife looked back and turned to a pillar of salt.

Lots wife is an example from which we can learn. Each person is accountable for his own actions. Even the destruction of Sodom is an example. "And turning the cities of Sodom and Gomorrah into ashes, condemned them to destruction, making them and example to those who afterward would live ungodly" (2 Peter 2:6).

One can live right in a wicked city. Lot lingered before leaving the city, but he did leave. "And delivered righteous Lot, who was oppressed by the filthy conduct of the wicked (for that righteous man, dwelling among them, tormented his righteous soul from day to day by seeing and hearing their lawless deeds" (2 Peter 2:7-8).

She was plainly warned. After being led outside by the angels, they were told not to look back (Genesis 19:17). We have also been warned of the consequences of sin. "For the wages of sin is death, but the gift of God is eternal life in Christ fJesus our Lord" (Romans 6:23).

She went part way but did not finish. After she was outside, she looked back and turned to a pillar of salt. To begin the race is not sufficient, we must run the race to the finish. We have a clear warning. "Beware, brethren, lest there be in any of you an evil heart of unbelief in departing from the living God"' (Hebrews 3:12).

God means what He says. He expects obedience, even if He says it only once. The angels used plain language, with no hidden meaning, when they were told not to look back. Those things regarding what to do to become a Christian and how to live a Christian life, are never given in veiled language, but are stated in plain simple language.

MOAB AND AMMON

The angels told Lot to "escape to the mountains, lest you be destroyed" (Genesis 19:17). Lot pleaded with the angels to let him go to the little city of Zoar, to which the angels agreed. Lot became afraid to stay in Zoar, so he and his two daughters went to the mountains and dwelt in a cave.

"Now the firstborn said to the younger, our father is old, and there is no man on the earth to come in to us as is the custom of all the earth. Come let us make our father drink wine, and we will lie with him, that we may preserve the linage of our father" (Genesis 19:311-32).

They made their father drunk and the firstborn lay with him. The next night they made their father drunk again and the younger daughter lay with him. As a result of this incest , the firstborn bore a son and named him Moab. Younger bore a son and called him Ben-Ammi. The Moabites and Ammonites came from these two sons.

Incest is having sexual intercourse with a close relative, which one is forbidden to marry. 1 Corinthians 5 deals with a church member who has his father's wife. The law forbids incest (Leviticus 18:6-18).

Balak, the king of Moab, hired Balaam to curse God's people but God turned it into a blessing (Numbers 22:1-20).

The women of Moab enticed the Israelites into a form of idolatry that involved sexual immorality, which brought punishment from God (Numbers 25:1-6). The events in the book of Ruth occurred during this period. Ruth was a Moabite and became an ancestor of David, and therefore of Christ (Ruth 2:6; 4:13-22; Matthew 1:5-16).

The Ammonites became enemies of Israel and joined forces with Jehoshaphat, but because God confused them, they destroyed themselves (2 Chronicles 20:1-23).

Because of the bad choice of Lot to pitch his tent toward Sodom, he lost part of his family in Sodom, he lost his wealth, his wife sinned and turned to a pillar of salt, and he had children by his own daughters.

CHAPTER 11 - ISAAC – A CHILD OF PROMISE

Isaac was one of several who were named before their birth, and some were named before they were conceived. Isaac (Genesis 17:19), Jesus (Luke 1:31; Matthew 1:21), John (Luke 1:13), Ishmael (Genesis 16:11), Solomon (1 Chronicles 22:9), and Josiah (1 Kings 13:2).

CHILD OF PROMISE

When Abraham was seventy-five years old God called Abraham and told him to leave his country and his family and go to the land He would show him. God would make him a great nation and that all families of the earth would be blessed through his seed.

At this time Abraham had no children. He asked God to accept Eleizer as his seed (Genesis 15:2-3), but God refused by asking him to count the stars, and saying that is the way his descendants would be.

Sarah had a maid named Hagar, and she suggested Abraham have children by her. Ishmael was born by her when Abraham was eighty six years old. When Abraham was ninety nine God appeared to Abraham again restated His promises, and promised Sarah would bear Isaac the next year. Abraham was a hundred years old and Sarah was ninety when Isaac was born, twenty five years after the original promise.

Abraham never doubted God, though he did not know how the promise would be fulfilled. "And not being weak in faith, he did not consider his own body, already dead (since he was about a hundred years old), and the deadness of Sarah's womb. He did not waver at the promise of God through unbelief, but was strengthened in faith, giving glory to God, and being fully convinced that what He had promised He was also able to perform." (Romans 4:19-21).

ISAAC AND ISHMAEL

At the time the birth announcement was given, Abraham asked that the seed would be counted through Ishmael, but God again refused.

"Then God said: No, Sarah your wife shall bear you a son, and you shall call his name Isaac; I will establish My covenant with him for an everlasting covenant, and with his descendants after him. And as for Ishmael, I have heard you. Behold, I have blessed him, and will make him fruitful, and will multiply him exceedingly. He shall beget twelve princes, and I will make him a great nation. But My covenant I will establish with Isaac, whom Sarah shall bear to you at this set time next year" (Genesis 17:19-21).

The Muslim claim that Ishmael is the one through whom the blessings of God will come is false, for twice in these three verses it is clearly stated that Isaac and not Ishmael is the one through whom God would bless the world. Isaac is the promised seed.

ABRAHAM IS TESTED

Abraham now knows that through Isaac God would fulfill His promise to bless the world. It is a real test of his faith when God told him to offer Isaac as a burnt offering. Abraham had such deep faith in God that he immediately prepared to obey God. The writer of Hebrews explains what Abraham was thinking.

"By faith Abraham, when he was tested, offered up Isaac, and he who had received the promises offered up his only begotten son, of whom it was said, In Isaac your seed shall be called, concluding that God was able to raise him up, even from the dead, from which he also received him in a figurative sense" (Hebrews 11:17-19).

The details of this event are recorded in Genesis 22. Abraham took Isaac, two servants, wood for the sacrifice, and went to the mountain God showed him. "And Abraham said to his young men, stay here with the donkey; the lad and I will go yonder and worship, and we will come back to you"" (Genesis 22:5).

Abraham and Isaac would "go yonder and worship". What he had been doing was not worship. We have instructions to do certain things in worship, so everything we do is not worship. In reply to the devil, Jesus quoted Deuteronomy 6:13. "You shall serve" (Matthew 4:10). Some things we do is worship aand some things is service. When the wise men came to Jerusalem to see the King of the Jews, they said we "have come to worship Him" (Matthew 2:2). What they had been doing was not worship. When we help the poor, sick and needy, we may serve God in doing so, but it is not worship.

AN ALLEGORY

When Jesus died on the cross, the law was abolished (Colossians 2:14; Ephesians 2:14-15), but there was always the danger in the early church of going back to the law, especially by requiring certain things. Gentiles were being taught they could become Christians but they must also be circumcised. "And certain men came down from Judea and taught the brethren, Unless you are circumcised according to the custom of Moses, you cannot be saved" (Acts 15:1).

Paul wrote, "Indeed, I Paul, say to you that if yoou become circumcised, Christ will profit you nothing. And I testify again to every man who becomes circumcised that he is a debtor to keep the whole law" (Galatians 5:2-3). If they go back to the law and bind part of it, there are serious consequences. 1) Christ will profit you nothing. 2) You are obligated to keep the whole law (including burnt offerings. 3) You have fallen from grace (verse 24).

Isaac and Sarah and Hagar and Ishmael are used to teach by an allegory that the law was taken away at the cross, and is not bound on us. Hagar and Ishmael represent the law given at Mount Sinai. Sarah and Isaac represent the law that went out from Jerusalem.

"For it is written that Abraham had two sons: the one by a bondwoman, the other by a freewoman. But he who was of the bondwoman was born according to the flesh, and he of the freewoman through promise, which things are symbolic. For these are the two covenants: the one from Mount Sinai which gives birth to bondage, which is Hagar" (Galatians 4:22-24). Ishmael was born after the flesh, that is, in the natural way, but Abraham and Sarah were old and Sarah had past the age of child bearing, but Isaac was born to her because of the promise of God.

Hagar, a bondwoman, represents the law. Sarah, a free woman, represents the gospel. "So then, brethren, we are not children of the bondwoman but of the free" (Galatians 4:31). It is clear we are not children of God by the law, but by the gospel.

REBEKAH BECOMES WIFE OF ISAAC

Abraham asked his oldest servant who ruled over everything he had, to go back to his country and his family and get a wife for Isaac. He made him swear he would not take a wife from the Canaanites, and that he would not take Isaac back to his country. Abraham recalled the promise God had made to him about the land.

"The Lord God of heaven who took me from my father's house and from the land of my family, and who spoke to me and swore to me, saying, to your descendants I give this land, He will send His angel before you, and you shall take a wife for my son from there" (Genesis 24:7). Isaac would inherit all that Abraham had (Genesis 24:36).

The servant took ten camels and went to Nahor a city in Mesopotamia.. He had the camels kneel down outside the city by the water well and waited for the women to come draw water in the evening. He prayed that when he asked one of the daughter's of the men of the city for a drink, that after he drank she would also give water for his camels to drink. When he asked Rebekah for a drink, she did exactly as he had asked the Lord.

He found out she was the daughter of Bethuel, Nahor's son, Abraham's brother. Her brother Laben came to the servant and brought him, his men and his camels to their house. They set food before them but the servant would not eat until he revealed his errand. The servant rehearsed every detail from the time Abraham had sent him, and how he had found Rebekah. Laban and Bethual agreed that what had happened was of the Lord, and they should take Rebekah and go to Isaac.

They were willing for her to go but wanted her to stay with them ten days. The servant said, "Do not hinder me, since the Lord has prospered my way, send me away so I may go to my master" (Genesis 24:56).

They called Rebekah to ask her personally, "will you go with this man?" And she said, "I will go." They sent her away with a blessing.

"Our sister, may you become
The mother of thousands of ten thousands;
And may your descendants possess
The gates of those who hate them.
(Genesis 24:60)

Isaac was forty years old when he took Rebekah as his wife (Genesis 25:20).

JACOB AND ESAU

"Now Isaac pleaded with the Lord for his wife, because she was barren; and the Lord granted his plea, and Rebekah conceived. But the children struggled together within her; and she said, If all is well, why am I like this? So she went to inquire of the Lord and the Lord said to her:

"Two nations are in your womb,
Two peoples shall be separated from your body;
One people shall be stronger than the other.
And the older shall serve the younger."
(Genesis 25:21-23).

Esau was born first and his brother took hold of his heel, whom they named Jacob which means "supplanter or deceitful." Esau was a hunter; Jacob was a mild man, dwelling in tents. Isaac loved Esau but Rebekah loved Jacob.

Jacob had cooked a stew, when Esau came in from the field and was weary, he ask Jacob for some of the stew. Jacob asked him to sell his birthright for some of the stew. "And Esau said, Look, I am about to die; so what is this birthright to me?"

(Genesis 25:32). He sold his birthright to him that day.

The writer of Hebrews recalls this event and the consequences of it. " Lest there be any fornicator or profane person like Esau, who for one morsel of food sold his birthright. For you know that afterward, when he wanted to inherit the blessing he was rejected, for he found no place for repentance, though he sought it diligently with tears" (Hebrews 12:16-17).

DECEPTION OF ISAAC

One day when Isaac was old and his eyes were dim, he asked Esau to take his bow and hunt for game and make him some savory food that he liked, and that he would bless him. Rebekah heard Isaac speak to Esau, so she planned for Jacob to receive the blessing.

Rebekah told Jacob to bring two choice goats and she would make savory food for Isaac. Since Esau was a hairy man and Jacob was smooth skinned, Jacob was afraid he would be discovered and he would receive a curse rather than a blessing. Rebekah put Esau's clothes on Jacob. She put skins of the goats on his hands and the smooth part of his neck.

"Jacob said to his father, I am Esau your firstborn; I have done just as you told me; please arise, sit and eat of the game, that your soul may bless me. But Isaac said to his son, How is it that you have found it so quickly, my son? And he said, because the Lord your God brought it to me." (Genesis 27:19-20). Isaac was deceived, he ate and blessed Jacob (Genesis 27:27-29).

As soon as Isaac had blessed Jacob, Esau came in from hunting and had made savory food for his father. He gave it to his father and asked for a blessing. Isaac realized he had been deceived and he had blessed Jacob instead of his firstborn.

Jacob received the blessing and the birthright. "So Esau hated Jacob because of the blessing with which his father blessed him, and Esau said in his heart, The days of mourning for my father are at hand; then I will kill my brother Jacob" (Genesis 27:41).

Isaac and Rebekah sent Jacob to her brother Laban in Haran until Esau's anger is turned away.

CHAPTER 12 - JACOB THE SUPPLANTER

When Jacob and Esau were born, Jacob took hold of the heel of Esau (Genesis 25:26), so his name was called Jacob, which means supplanter or deceitful. He seemed to live up to that name as he got the birthright, the blessing and the flocks at Laban's house.

THE BIRTHRIGHT

There were rights, privileges and possessions that usually went with the firstborn. He had a favored position and he received a double portion of his father's assets (Deuteronomy 21:15-17). The firstborn would also have a blessing from the father (Genesis 27:27). "Their father gave them great gifts of silver and gold and precious things with fortified cities in Judah; but he gave the kingdom to Jehoram, because he was the firstborn. (2 Chronicles 21:3).

The firstborn could live in a way as to forfeit these

blessings. Esau sold his birthright for some stew when he was hungry (Genesis 25:29-34). Reuben lost his birthright because of incest with Bilhah, his father's concubine (Genesis 35:22; 1 Chronicles 5:1).

Christ has that honored position of being the firstborn. "And He is the head of the body, the church, who is the beginning, the firstborn from the dead, that in all things He may have the preeminence" (Colossians 1:18). He was the first to rise to die no more (Romans 6:9). In this sense He is the firstborn. Israel was not the first nation in the world, but she is given that place of being the firstborn (Jeremiah 31:9).

Isaac intended to give a blessing to Esau the firstborn, but through deceit he blessed Jacob instead of Esau (Genesis 27:1-29).

JACOB GOES TO LABAN

When Esau learned Jacob had received the blessing, he planned to kill him after the death of their father. So Jacob would not take a wife from the daughters of Heth, his parents sent him to the house of Bethuel so he could take a wife from the daughters of Laban, the brother of Rebekah. This would also give time for the anger of Esau to turn away from Jacob.

Laban had two daughters – Leah and Rachel. Leah was the oldest and she had weak eyes. Rachel was "beautiful of form and appearance" (Genesis 29:17). Jacob loved Rachel and agreed to work for Laban for seven years for Rachel to be his wife.

When the time came Laban deceived Jacob and gave Leah instead of Rachel. Jacob did not know until the next morning. Laban said in their country, they could not give the younger before the firstborn. Jacob agreed to work seven more years for Rachel.

A Topical Study of Genesis

JACOB LEAVES LABAN

His first attempt to leave resulted in another agreement to stay (Genesis 30:26-28). Jacob agreed to take certain animals as his wages. "Let me pass through all your flock today, removing from there all the speckled and spotted sheep, and all the brown ones among the lambs, and the spotted and speckled among the goats; and these shall be my wages" (Genesis 30:32).

Through selective breeding Jacob accumulated large flocks and herds, and became very prosperous. Laban changed his attitude toward Jacob, so the Lord told Jacob to return to his family in the land of his father. On his way to Laben he spent the night at Bethel where he had a dream in which the Lord told he would inherit that land and that through his seed "all the families of the earth would be blessed" (Genesis 28:14). This is the same promise Abraham and Isaac had received (Genesis 12:1-3; 26:4).

Jacob knew Laban would not let him leave peacefully, so he called Rachel and Leah and told them his plan. "And you know that with all my might I have served your father. Yet your father has deceived me and changed my wages ten times, but God did not allow him to hurt me" (Genesis 31:6-7).

While Laban had gone to shear his sheep, Jacob took his family and all of his animals to flee from Laban. Laban learned about it and came after Jacob, but after discussion Laban left and went back to his own place. Jacob had served him twenty years (Genesis 31:38, 41).

On his way back to Canaan, "Jacob was left alone; and a Man wrestled with him until the break of day" (Genesis 32:24). Jacob said, "I will not let you go unless you bless me!" So He said to him, what is your name? He said, Jacob. And He said, "Your name shall no longer be called Jacob, but Israel; for you have struggled with God and with men, and have prevailed" (Genesis 32:26-28).

The twelve tribes are the children of Israel, and the

descendents of Abraham. God is keeping his promise to Abraham to make him a great nation.

JACOB AND ESAU MEET

When Jacob left his father's house, Esau had planned to kill him because he had taken the birthright and the blessing. He is afraid of Esau and asks the Lord for protection (Genesis 32:11). He arranged a present for Esau. He divided the animals and people for protection when they met Esau.

As it turned out there was no need to fear Esau, and they embraced and received each other (Genesis 33:4).

JOSEPH SOLD BY HIS BROTHERS

When Joseph was seventeen there began a series of serious troubles in his life. His father loved him more than all his brothers and made him a coat of many colors. He had dreams that meant his brothers would bow down to him, so they hated him and sold him as a slave into Egypt. He was lied about and put into prison. The butler forgot him, but eventually he was made next to the king in power.

Pharaoh had dreams and no one could tell him the meaning. It was at this time the butler remembered Joseph interpreted his dream in prison. They sent for Joseph to give the meaning of Pharaoh's dream. His dream meant there would be seven years of plenty followed by seven years of famine. Joseph was selected to collect grain during the seven years of plenty, and later to sell it during the famine.

"And Pharaoh said to his servants, can we find such a one as this man in whom is the Spirit of God? Then Pharaoh said to Joseph, Inasmuch as God has shown you all this, there is no one as discerning and wise as you. You shall be over my house, and all my people shall be ruled according to your word; only in regard to the throne will I be greater than you" (Genesis 41:38-40).

FAMINE OVER THE LAND

The famine extended beyond Egypt, for Canaan was affected by it. When Jacob heard there was grain in Egypt, he sent ten sons there to buy grain. When they got there, their brother, Joseph, was in charge of selling the grain. He knew them and could understand all they said, though they did not recognize them.

The last place they would have expected to see Joseph would be second in command in Egypt, for they sold him as a slave. He spoke to them through an interpreter, so they would not have thought of him. Also, it had been fifteen years since they had seen him (Genesis 37:2; 41:46; 45:6).

After a time Joseph reveals himself to them and tells them there will be five more years of the famine. He instructs them to bring their father Jacob to Egypt because of the famine.

JACOB GOES TO EGYPT

Seventy people went to Egypt (Genesis 46:27), when Jacob was on hundred and thirty years old (Genesis 47:9). God told Jacob that Joseph "will put his hands on your eyes" (Genesis 46:4). This meant he would close his eyes when he died. He lived in Egypt seventeen years and died at age one hundred forty seven (Genesis 47:28).

Jacob asked Joseph not to bury him in Egypt. He was embalmed by the physicians in Egypt, and carried back to Canaan and buried in the cave in the field of Machpelah, as he requested.

Albert Gardner

JACOB BLESSES HIS CHILDREN

When the Promised Land was divided, the tribe of Levi, the priestly tribe, did not receive land. The two sons of Joseph, Ephraim and Manasseh, took the place of Joseph and Levi, which make twelve. Jacob blessed them like they were his own children (Genesis 48:5-6).

Jacob tells each of his sons what will befall them. Reuben, the firstborn, did not receive the blessing because he had defiled his father's bed. Of special interest is the blessing of Judah. "The scepter shall not depart from Judah, nor a lawgiver from between his feet until Shiloh comes; and to Him shall be the obedience of the people" (Genesis 49:10).

Jesus is the lawgiver that came from the tribe of Judah. We can see the care, protection, and guidance God gave to His people, especially to the tribe of Judah. Joseph went to Egypt to "preserve life. He gave that as his purpose for being in Egypt (Genesis 45:5). He preserved physical life, but more importantly, he preserved spiritual life by saving Judah through whom the Messiah would be born.

CHAPTER 13 - THE TRIALS OF JOSEPH

Joseph was the favorite son of the favorite wife of Jacob and this was a source of some of his troubles. Some problems are self made, while other trials come through circumstances with which we had nothing to do.

No one is exempt. We ought to be thankful for trials (James 1:2-3), knowing that trials are designed to purify us. They build character when we overcome them. "In this you greatly rejoice, though now for a little while, if need be, you have been grieved by various trials, that the genuineness of your faith, being much more precious than gold that perishes, though it is tested by fire, may be found to praise, honor, and glory at the revelation of Jesus Christ " (1 Peter 1:6-7).

The book of Job tells about a good man who had severe trials put on him by the devil, which God allowed to test his faith. When it was over Job said "I have heard of You by the hearing of the ear, but now my eyes see You. Therefore, I abhor myself, and repent in dust and ashes" (Job 42:5-6).

Abraham was tested (Genesis 22:1), when he was told to offer Isaac as a sacrifice. He passed the test. The Angel of the Lord said, *Do not lay hour hand on the lad, or do anything to him; for now I know that you fear God, since you have not withheld your son, your only son, from me" (Genesis 22:12).

Early Christians suffered in ways we can hardly imagine (Hebrews 10:32-35). First Peter was written to comfort Christians who were suffering. "But let none of you suffer as a murderer, a thief, an evildoer, or as a busybody in other people's matters. Yet if anyone suffers as a Christian, let him not be ashamed, but let him glorify God in this matter" (1 Peter 4:15-16).

Trials are for our good. Paul says we rejoice in hope, and in tribulations "knowing that tribulations produces perseverance; and perseverance, character; and character, hope" (Romans 5:2-4). We ought to be thankful for anything or to anybody that will help us go to heaven. Paul says these trials "work for us". "For our light affliction, which is but for a moment, is working for us a far more exceeding and eternal weight of glory" (2 Corinthians 4:17).

The apostle Paul listed many things he suffered because he was a Christian (2 Corinthians 11:23-28). Of course, the perfect example of suffering is Jesus Christ our Lord, "who when He was reviled, did not revile in return; when He suffered, He did not threaten, but committed Himself to Him who judges righteously; who Himself bore our sins in His own body on the tree, that we having died to sins, might live for righteousness – by whose stripes you were healed" (1 Peter 2:23-24).

Isaiah foretold the suffering of Christ. "He is despised and rejected by men, a Man of sorrows and acquainted with grief. And we hid, as it were, our faces from Him; He was despised, and we did not esteem Him. Surely He has borne our griefs and carried our sorrows; Yet we esteemed Him stricken, smitten by God, and afflicted. But He was wounded for our transgressions, He was bruised for our iniquities; The chastisement for our peace was upon Him, and by His stripes we are healed. All we like sheep have gone astray; We have turned, every one, to his own way; and the Lord has laid on Him the iniquity of us all " (Isaiah 53:3-6).

PARTIALITY OF HIS FATHER

"Now Israel loved Joseph more than all his children, because he was the son of his old age. Also he made him a tunic of many colors" (Genesis 37:3).

Because each personality is different, parents may love them differently, but with Joseph partiality produced hatred, envy and even the thought of murder. Well meaning parents can be the source of much heartache.

Joseph told his dreams about the bowing sheaves and the stars bowing to him (Genesis 37:7-10). This caused even more hatred.

SOLD BY HIS BRETHREN

Jacob sent Joseph to check on his brothers who were feeding their father's flock in Shechem. When they saw him "they conspired against him to kill him." They put him in a pit and took his coat of many colors. Instead of killing him as they first thought, they sold him to Medianite traders for twenty shekels of silver, and they took Joseph to Egypt.

In order to cover their terrible deed, they took his coat and dipped it in the blood of a goat in order to deceive their father. When they took it back to Jacob he concluded, "a wild beast has devoured him. Without doubt Joseph is torn to pieces" (Genesis 37:33). For many years he mourned for the false belief that Joseph was dead.

It is possible to be honestly mistaken. Jacob experienced the emotions of mourning and weeping as if it were true. He was honest and sincere, but he was wrong. Saul of Tarsus was honestly mistaken. He said, "I have lived in all good conscience before God until this day" (Acts 23:1). Later, he admitted he had been wrong, "although I was formerly a blasphemer, a persecutor, and an insolent man; but I obtained mercy because

I did it ignorantly in unbelief" (1 Timothy 1:13).

Much error is taught and many honestly follow false teaching. Many reject the necessity of baptism for salvation (1 Peter 3:21). Great numbers accept salvation by faith only (James 2:24). The masses of people are members of denominations they cannot read about in the Bible, which says there is one body (Ephesians 1:22-23; 4:4-6; 5:23).

Knowing it is possible to be honestly mistaken, we should follow the teaching of 1 Thessalonians 5: 21. "Test all things; hold fast what is good". Every doctrine, belief, and practice should be tested by the word of God. Reject what does not match up. Hold on to truth.

TEMPTED BY A WICKED WOMAN

Joseph was sold to Potiphar, an officer of Pharaoh, Captain of the guard in Egypt. Pharoah soon learned that Joseph was successful, trustworthy and that all things seemed to prosper under his authority. Everything in his house was turned over to Joseph, so Pharoah did not know what was in his house except the bread he ate.

The wife of Pharaoh asked Joseph to lie with her and he refused. "There is no one greater in this house than I, nor has he pept back anything from me but you, because you are his wife. How then can I do this great wickedness and sin against God?" (Genesis 39:9).

She constantly day by day asked that he commit adultery with her. Though he was past seventeen when his sex drive would have been strong, he refused to sin with her. One day when he was doing his work in the house, and no one was in the house, she caught his garment to force him, he ran outside leaving his garment in her hand. She told the men of the house that Joseph had tried to force her and used his garment to prove it.

When Pharaoh came home she told the same lie to him and he believed her. Pharoah had Joseph put in the prison where the king's prisoners were kept. Even in the prison a position of favor with the keeper of the prison was given to Joseph.

What Potiphar's wife wanted to do, Joseph called wickedness and sin. Many are so tolerant today that they see nothing wrong with it. They are much like the people in Isaiah's day. "Woe to those who call evil good, and good evil; who put darkness for light, and light for darkness; who put bitter for sweet, and sweet for bitter" (Isaiah 5:20).

It is normal and natural for men and women to be attracted to each other. Were it not so there would be no reproduction and the human race would die out. God made it that way, but teaches us sexual activity is to be satisfied within marriage (1 Corinthians 7:1-5).

"Marriage is honorable among all, and the bed undefiled; but fornicators and adulterers God will judge" (Hebrews 13:4). Sex before marriage is sin, and sex with someone other than your spouse (and this includes homosexuality) is sin. Joseph knew this and refused to sin.

JOSEPH WENT TO PRISON

Potiphar's wife lied about Joseph and he went to prison for something he did not do. He is suffering as an innocent man. Life is sometimes unfair. One after another, it seems like Joseph has a bad break in life. His home life was filled with hatred and envy. His brothers sold him as a slave. Potiphar's wife lied about him, and he is now in prison.

Because the Lord was with Joseph, he received special favor from the keeper and Joseph was put in charge and all was done under his authority. In the prison at that time were the baker and butler of the king of Egypt. Each of them had dreams and Joseph gave the interpretation of their dreams. In times past God revealed His will to people through dreams, angels, visions, and even directly. He no longer speaks to people that way but "has in these last days spoken to us by His Son" (Hebrews 1:2) His Son speaks through the written word

(John 12:48-50; Ephesians 3:3-5; 1 Corinthians 4:6).

The dream of the butler meant he would be restored to his former place of serving the king. Joseph asked a favor of him. "But remember me when it is well with you, and please show kindness to me; make mention of me to Pharaoh, and get me out of this house" (Genesis 40:14), but he forgot him, another bad break.

REACHED THE TOP AT THIRTY

Joseph left home at seventeen (Genesis 37:2), and he was thirty years old when he stood before Pharaoh to interpret his dreams (Genesis 41:46).. He had been down to the bottom in many ways but now Pharaoh puts him in charge as the second in command over all the land of Egypt.

This also is a real test. One day he is a prisoner and the next day he is next to the king. Rapid rise in wealth or status often ruins people. They cannot handle it. They may forget God, forsake the church, desert family and friends.

When Pharaoh had dreams, the butler remembered Joseph and mentioned him to the king. Joseph was released from prison and brought before the king to interpret his dreams. Joseph told him his dreams meant there would be seven years of plenty followed by seven years of famine. He advised the king to collect one-fifth of the produce of the land during the plentiful years so there would be food during the famine.

Joseph was chosen to collect and distribute the food. He gathered so much that they finally stopped counting. The famine extended to other countries, so they came to Egypt to buy grain during the famine.

JOSEPH MEETS HIS BROTHERS

If anyone ever had a right to be bitter and to seek revenge,

Joseph did. He is now face to face with those who hated him enough to consider murder, but instead sold him as a slave. This led him to be wrongfully imprisoned, lied about, and forgotten by one who should have remembered him.

Now he is in position of authority and could really do harm to those who hurt him. They had hindered him for thirteen years. Jacob had sent ten sons to Egypt to buy food because the famine had extended to Canaan. Joseph recognized his brothers but the last place they would have expected to see Joseph would be almost like the king in Egypt. They did not know him, for he spoke through an interpreter (Genesis 42:23). Joseph had been in Egypt thirteen years and knew their language well, but he also could understand every word they spoke.

These brothers remembered their cruel deed of selling Joseph and believed their problems were connected to it. "Then they said to one another, we are truly guilty concerning our brother, for we saw the anguish of his soul when he pleaded with us, and we would not hear; therefore this distress has come upon us" (Genesis 42:21). They did literally bow down to Joseph as his bowing sheaves indicated in his dream while he was still at home. Many details of the life of Joseph are not included here, but one should read Genesis 37-50.

Finally Joseph makes himself known to his brothers and asks them to bring their father there because there would still be five years of famine. He clears everyone out of the room except his brothers. "And he wept aloud, and the Egyptians and the house of Pharaoh heard it. Then Joseph said to his brothers, 'I am Joseph; does my father still live?' But his brothers could not answer him, for they were dismayed in his presence. And Joseph said to his brothers 'Please come near to me.' So they came near. Then he said: 'I am Joseph your brother, whom you sold into Egypt. But now, do not therefore be grieved or angry with yourselves because you sold me here; for God sent me before you to preserve life' " (Genesis 45:2-5).

TWO SONS

It is not revealed what Joseph was thinking immediately after he was sold by his brothers, or whether he thought his father would come for him. He did not know what his brothers had told their father.

The names of his two sons are significant. "Joseph called the name of the firstborn Manesseh: For God has made me forget all my toil and all my father's house and the name of the second he called Ephraim: For God has caused me to be fruitful in the land of my affliction:: (Genesis 41:51-52).

Our trials may not be that we are sold into slavery, but they will be real as we face them. We must know that they will work to our good (Romans 8:28), and that they will not be more than we can bear (1 Corinthians 10:13).

Young people area to remember their creator in the days of their youth (Ecclesiastes 12:1). God was with Joseph throughout his life, even when he was on his death bed. "By faith Joseph, when he was dying, made mention of the departure of the children of Israel, and gave instructions concerning his bones" (Hebrews 11:22; see Genesis 50:24-26).

CHAPTER 14 - SOME WOMEN IN GENESIS

We have seen in our study of this great book, that some women have had a very important part in the plan of God.

Some women are not named. Some are in the background and almost nothing is said of them. Since genealogy is traced through the men, the emphasis has not been on women, but that does not mean their work is unimportant.

Women have been valuable in the church and in the spread of the gospel. Such names as Dorcas, Pricilla, Pheba come to mind, as well as those who are unnamed. Their role is not as preachers, but they have a supporting role which is necessary and is very important (Romans 16:1-2).

EVE

Adam named the animals, and there was not found one suitable to him for companionship and procreation. God said, " it is good" about His creation until He made man. "And the Lord God said, It is not good that man should be alone; I will make him a helper comparable to him" (Genesis 2:18).

God caused a deep sleep to fall on Adam. He took a rib

from his side and made a woman. And brought her to Adam, and he said, "This is now bone of my bones and flesh of my flesh; she shall be called Woman, because she was taken out of man" (Genesis 2:23). Another reason he called her Eve was "she was the mother of all living" (Genesis 3:20).

"That the woman was made of a rib out of the side of Adam, not taken out of his head to rule over him, nor out of his feet to be trampled upon by him, but out of his side to be equal with him, under his arm to be protected, and near his heart to be beloved" (Matthew Henry).

Eve was the other half. She completed him. She is suitable. She compliments him. She came from man and for man (1 Corinthians 11:8-9). She is comparable to him. Man alone and left to himself becomes hard, rash and insensitive. When women become that way the home and society suffers.

THE HOME

Marriage is approved and regulated by God, since He pronounced the first couple husband and wife. From the beginning of the creation God made them male and female (Matthew 19:4; Mark 10:6), and intended that one man and one woman should live together until death. He approved of sex within marriage (Hebrews 13:4), but it never entered His mind to have same sex marriages, and condemned homosexuality (Romans 1:24-27). God's order is clear. "But I want you to know that the head of every man is Christ, the head of woman is man, and the head of Christ is God" (1 Corinthians 11:3). The idea that the husband is the head of his wife is not stated because that is the way it was in culture at that time. Paul does not connect this teaching to culture but to creation (1 Corinthians 11:9).

"Let a woman learn in silence with all submission, and I do not permit a woman to teach or to have authority over a man, but to be in silence. For Adam was formed first, then Eve" (1 Timothy 2:11-13). Again, Paul connects this teaching to creation.

There is ample teaching about how the husband is to love, care for and protect his wife (Ephesians 5:23-25). He should never be harsh, domineering and hateful as he leads his family. With proper love for his wife, she will not find it difficult to submit to him.

ORIGIN OF SIN

The serpent deceived Eve (2 Corinthians 11:3). She heard, believed and obeyed a lie. She ate of the forbidden tree, and she gave to Adam and he ate, though he was not deceived (1 Timothy 2:14). She was tempted through "the lust of the flesh, the lust of the eyes, and the pride of life" (1 John 2:16).

The serpent was cursed and would be on his belly and eat of the dust of the ground. The woman would endure pain in child bearing. Adam was told the ground would be cursed. It would bring forth thorns and thistles (Genesis 3:14-19).

SEED PROMISE

Though the seed promise was enlarged when it is stated to Abraham (Genesis 12:1-3), it is given first in Genesis 3:15. "And I will put enmity between you and the woman, and between your seed and her Seed; He shall bruise your head, and you shall bruise His heel."

This promise is not to show that in the future women would be afraid of snakes, but is at least a veiled promise of Christ, for He is the only one who is the seed of a woman without a human father. "But when the fullness of the time had come, God sent forth His Son, born of a woman, born under the law" (Galatians 4:4; see Luke 1:30-35).

Satan would give a minor blow when he would bruise the heel of Jesus by the crucifixion, but Christ would give a mortal blow to Satan's head when He was raised from the dead.

It was through Eve that sin entered, it was also through woman a savior was born.

KETURAH

After the death of Sarah, Abraham took a wife named Keturah (Genesis 25:1). She is also called Abraham's concubine (1 Chronicles 1:32). She had six sons by Abraham, but none of them were on the level with Isaac.

RACHEL AND LEAH

She was the daughter of Laban, who was a brother of Rebekah.

They were daughters of Laban. Laban and Rebekah were brother and sister. Jacob, the son of Isaac and Rebekah, was sent to Laban's house to seek a wife.

Jacob stayed with Laban and Laban offered him wages to stay and work for him. Jacob agreed to work for him for seven years if he would give him his daughter, Rachel, for his wife. After working seven years he asked for his wife. Instead of Rachel, Laban gave Leah and he did not know he had been deceived until the next morning. Laban said in that country the younger could not be given before the firstborn. He had to work seven more years for Rachel.

<u>Children by Rachel;</u> Joseph and Benjamin

<u>Children by Bilhah, Rachel's maid;</u> Dan and Naphtali

<u>Children by Leah;</u> Reuben, Simeon, Levi, Judah, Issachar, Zebulun, and a daughter, Dinah.

<u>Children by Zilpah, Leah's maid;</u> Gad and Asher.

These twelve sons of Jacob became the twelve tribes of Israel.

LOT'S WIFE

She is not named. Jesus simply said, "Remember Lot's wife" (Luke 17:32). When Sodom was destroyed, Lot and his family was told by the angel not to look back. Lot's wife looked back and turned into a pillar of salt. She is an example of punishment for the disobedient.

HAGAR

Ten years after God promised Abraham He would make of him a great nation, Abraham still had no children. God had refused to count the seed through Eliezer, and told him it would be his own son (Genesis 15:1-5).

Sarah had an Egyptian maid named Hagar, whom she told Abraham to take as his wife and bear children by her. He agreed, and at age eighty six Ishmael was born to them."

Hagar despised Sarah, and Sarah dealt harshly with her, so she fled from her. The Angel of the Lord found her in the wilderness and told her to return to Sarah and submit to her. "And the Angel of the Lord said to her: Behold, you are with child, and yoou shall bear a son. You shall call his name Ishmael, because the Lord has heard your affliction. He shall be a wild man; his hand shall be against every man, and every man's hand against him. And he shall dwell in the presence of all his brethren" (Genesis 16:11-12).

God told Abraham that Sarah would bear a son and his name would be Isaac and he would be the one through whom He would bless all nations. He said Ishmael would be a great nation "but My Covenant I will establish with Isaac, whom Sarah shall bear to you at this set time next year" (Genesis 17:21).

The apostle Paul uses Hagar and Sarah and their sons, to teach by way of an allegory that we are not under the Old Covenant. Hagar represents the law given at Mount Sinai, and Sarah represents the gospel that went forth from Jerusalem. He concludes, "So then, brethren, we are not children of the bondwoman but of the free" (Galatians 4:31).

REBEKAH

Rebekah was the daughter of Bethuel, the son of Nahar, Abraham's brother (Genesis 24:15). This would mean Abraham would be her great uncle, and that Isaac would be her second cousin.

Abraham made his servant sware he would not take a wife for Isaac from the daughters of the Canaanites, but would go to his country and his family and get a wife for him. Genesis 24 records the details of the search for a wife, and how Rebekah was chosen.

Twin boys Jacob and Esau, were born to them twenty years after they married (Genesis 25:20, 26). Esau sold his birthright to Jacob for some food. Rebekah helped Jacob deceive his father Isaac, to receive a blessing, which was meant for Esau.

SARAH

Sarah was a half sister of Abraham. Abraham told Abimelech, "She is my sister", and he took her. God revealed to him in a dream that Sarah was a man's wife. Abraham said, "But indeed she is truly my sister. She is the daughter of my father, but not the daughter of my mother; and she became my wife" (Genesis 20:12).

God changed her name from Sarai to Sarah (Genesis 17:15). She was sixty-five when God promised Abraham through his seed all the families of the earth would be blessed.

She was ninety when she was told she would have Isaac in the next year. Abraham was a hundred years old. Sarah laughed (Genesis 17:17), because she was past the age of child bearing. This is why Isaac is called a child of promise.

Sarah died at age one hundred twenty seven (Genesis 23:1), and was buried in the cave of Machpelah which Abraham had bought from Ephron as a burial place. Sarah is the only woman whose age at her death is stated in the Bible.

Christian women are to follow the example of the life of Sarah. "For in this manner, in former times, the holy women who trusted in God also adorned themselves, being submissive to their own husbands, as Sarah obeyed Abraham, calling him lord, whose daughters you are if you do good and are not afraid with any terror" (1 Peter 3:5-6).

"By faith Sarah herself also received strength to conceive seed, and she bare a child when she was past the age, because she judged Him faithful who had promised" (Hebrews 11:11).

Albert Gardner

ABOUT THE AUTHOR

William Albert Gardner, Sr., (1928-2012) was born on Nov. 12, 1928, in Marmaduke, Ark., to Omar and Edna Sutton Gardner Rowe.

In May of 1948, he married his sweetheart and love of his life, Johnnie Frances Eades, of Kennett.

After completing high school at Marmaduke, Albert attended the College of Watchmaking at Memphis, Tenn., and in Kansas City, Mo. Albert worked at Collins Jewelry Store in Kennett, Paragould Jewelry Store in Arkansas and owned a jewelry store in Campbell, Mo. He entered Abilene Christian University and later Freed Hardeman University where he graduated earning a degree in Biblical Studies. Albert completed his Bachelor of Education degree from the University of Nebraska in Omaha, and later earned his Masters of Missions from Luther Rice Seminary.

Albert made the decision early on in his life to serve the Lord. He first started sharing the gospel at the Bakerville Church of Christ, east of Kennett, and ended his 62 years of service also with the Bakerville congregation. Albert served as a full time pulpit minister throughout several congregations both state side and in the foreign mission fields of Ghana, West Africa, South Africa, Belarus and in India, where he made over 20 trips sharing God's word. Albert was instrumental in setting up several Schools of Preaching in India.

Albert produced a radio program on KCRV and had radio programs in the local media nearly everywhere he worked. Albert held revival meetings in countless locations over his preaching career and was always ready to share the Gospel of Christ at every opportunity.

Albert had the opportunity to share God's Word through his writings for the Gospel Advocate, the Firm Foundation, and other publications. Albert was also a prolific author, having written over 22 published books, plus numerous religious pamphlets with each of these books also being translated into several India languages to be used in the India Mission field.

Albert became acquainted with Ham Radio while in the mission field and was an avid Ham Radio operator for over 50 years, holding an Extra Class license. Talking on the radio each morning was a part of his daily routine.

Albert and Frances have five children, 13 grandchildren, seven great-grandchildren, and several nieces and nephews. Albert's brother is E. Claude Gardner, of Henderson, Tenn., former President of Freed-Hardeman College.

Made in the USA
Middletown, DE
18 February 2019